Geoffrey Chaucer

'Along with its other mind-broadening features, this introduction offers a timely reminder that Chaucer benefited from a Europe-wide perspective and continues to evoke creative responses across cultures and borders.'

Nick Havely, University of York

'Already an eminent scholar of medieval literature, David Wallace now offers a thoroughly fresh engagement with Chaucer that will entice first-time readers even as it provokes new thought among established Chaucer hands. In nimble and unpretentious prose, he gives us Chaucer as a Londoner and founder of literary English but also as a fully involved European, a Catholic of comprehensive religiosity, a writer of his moment wide open to the future and the world.'

Paul Strohm, author, *The Poet's Tale*

Geoffrey Chaucer

A New Introduction

DAVID WALLACE

OXFORD

UNIVERSITY PRESS

OXFORD
UNIVERSITY PRESS

Great Clarendon Street, Oxford, OX2 6DP,
United Kingdom

Oxford University Press is a department of the University of Oxford.
It furthers the University's objective of excellence in research, scholarship,
and education by publishing worldwide. Oxford is a registered trade mark of
Oxford University Press in the UK and in certain other countries

First Edition published in 2017

Impression: 1

Published in the United States of America by Oxford University Press
198 Madison Avenue, New York, NY 10016, United States of America

British Library Cataloguing in Publication Data
Data available

Library of Congress Control Number: 2017932615

ISBN 978-0-19-880506-9

Printed in Great Britain by
Clays Ltd, St Ives plc

for Elaine Nixon

CONTENTS

ACKNOWLEDGEMENTS

Writing and rewriting this little book has been a pleasure from beginning to end. Andrea Keegan commissioned it, Jenny Nugee saw it through, Brian North copy-edited adroitly, and I owe much to all three. Further thanks are due to the teachers who fostered my love of Chaucer, from grammar school to grad school, and to all who have read Chaucer with me over the years. The New Chaucer Society, welcoming everyone to its biennial conferences, has for decades been my intellectual home from home. OUP's anonymous readers offered outstanding critiques, urging me to do better and bolder. Nick Havely (York), Daniel Davies (Penn), and Elaine Nixon (Jerusalem) also read generously and responded pointedly. This *piccolo libretto* is dedicated, in friendship, to Elaine.

ACKNOWLEDGEMENTS

LIST OF ILLUSTRATIONS

LIST OF ABBREVIATIONS

BL	British Library
CT	*The Canterbury Tales*
GP	*General Prologue to The Canterbury Tales*
HF	*The House of Fame*
LGW	*The Legend of Good Women*
ODNB	*The Oxford Dictionary of National Biography*
PF	*The Parliament of Fowls*
SGGK	*Sir Gawain and the Green Knight*
T&C	*Troilus and Criseyde*

1

Beginnings

Geoffrey Chaucer is a medieval poet enjoying a global renaissance. Why do poets, translators, and audiences from so many cultures, from the mountains of Iran to the islands of Japan, find Chaucer so inspiring? In current global conditions, when English has conquered the world, it is perhaps refreshing to encounter a writer *struggling* to convince the world that poetry and science, tragedy and astrology, could all be explored through English. French was still England's aristocratic language of choice when Chaucer was born, just before the catastrophic plague of 1348; Latin was used for university education, theological discussion, and for burying the dead. Could a hybrid tongue such as English, washed by waves of foreign invasion, ever generate great writing to compare with French and Italian? Chaucer, miraculously, thought that it could. And perhaps intuited that he had an opportunity that comes only once in any given language: to write afresh, inventively, without worrying about burdens of precedent, of 'sounding like' (without at first realizing it) some past master. Reading and working with Chaucer, so contemporary poet Lavinia Greenlaw says, is like meeting with English before the paint has dried.

First encounters with Chaucer for many people, sad to say, are often their last—especially when assigned to read, for examination purposes, the *General Prologue* to the *Canterbury Tales*. For the most part, *GP* is repetitious, necessarily so, with its gallery of pilgrim portraits. Much of *GP*'s specialized vocabulary, associated with particular trades, professions, and avocations, will not appear again, and so is soon forgotten. Better to pair the reading of each portrait with its tale, always with the understanding that no tale simply 'illustrates' the character of its pilgrim teller. The great exception to such repetitiveness in *GP* comes, of course, at the very beginning. Here Chaucer does something that will be found exceptional not just within *GP*, or *CT*, but anywhere in his writings. That is, he foregrounds himself as poetic virtuoso:

> Whan that Aprill with his shoures soote   *sweet showers*
> The droghte of March hath perced to the roote   *dryness*   *pierced*
>
> (1.1–2)

The opening 'when' here, situating us at a specific cosmic juncture, looks to coordinate with a 'then' which will tell of everything flowing from this moment:

> Thanne longen folk to goon on pilgrimages   *long*   *go*
>
> (1.12)

'Then', once found in line 12, pairs immediately with the sentence's main verb, *longen*. It is instructive, as a creative writing exercise, to choose any main verb, and then to try and reach it across twelve lines of poetry. It is not easy to sustain focus, to say nothing of sense, across banked rows of parallel and subordinate clauses. Certainly, Chaucer's self-appointed heir in English poetry, the Benedictine monk John Lydgate, could not do it: the opening of his *Siege of Thebes*, written to prequel Chaucer's *Knight's Tale*, never does find its main verb. Chaucer, however, having spoken of planetary motion, inspiring wind, natural regeneration, and birdsong, hits *longen* and then goes on to tell how humans, too, are stirred to move in springtime. He rounds out this epical first sentence at line 18 by rhyming 'seke' with 'seeke', employing the fancy effect of *rime riche* (rhyming two words which sound alike, but mean differently—here 'seek' and 'sick'). And then, in the very next couplet, he introduces himself:

> Bifel that in that seson on a day   *It happened*   *season*
> In Southwerk at the Tabard as I lay   *Southwark*   *Tabard Inn*
> (1.19–20)

To say that Chaucer 'introduces himself' here is paradoxical, since we have been in his company all along. First we meet him as poet, and then twenty lines later as 'I', another pub-dwelling pilgrim who will serve as our first-person correspondent for the duration. We must distinguish, then, the poet who begins *CT* as a virtuoso, with every line and rhyme inspiring confidence, from the pilgrim 'I' Chaucer who is not (we soon discover) the sharpest knife in the medieval pantry. And to wonder how both these Chaucers relate to the historical G. Chaucer, Esquire, is to wade still deeper into complications.

Designing Poetry

Another person vital to Chaucerian poetry, constitutive of it, is you, the reader. Every book loves and fears its readers, but

Chaucer is as finely attuned to audience reactions inside and outside his text-worlds as any dramatist: one of many reasons why Shakespeare loved Chaucer so much, and learned so much from him. Chaucer's poetry has designs on its readers, stirring strong emotions. At the same time, it (here generally with Chaucer speaking as an 'I') is keen to deny responsibility for any views or opinions raised, or conclusions reached, *especially* if preceded by strong emotions. 'Don't blame me' and 'I cannot say' ('Blameth nat me', 'Can I nat seyn'), phrases not often found in poetry, are characteristically Chaucerian. Responsibility for drawing conclusions is routinely thrown onto readerly shoulders. Chaucer is notoriously bad at closure, at completing the sentence *from this we have learned*...His *Clerk's Tale* offends worst of all. At line 1142, closure seems imminent as the Clerk says 'This storie is seyd' [so that . . .]. But by the time we reach 1212, seventy lines later, we have passed through so many closures and counter-closures that we have no idea what *that* was all about—beyond the bare facts of a lordly husband testing and torturing his peasant wife.

Similar confusions abound at the end of the *Physician's Tale*, an egregiously brief saga that sees a teenage girl in ancient Rome killed by her highly principled, aristocratic father (Figure 1). The father, named and rhymed in the first couplet, is Virginius; the daughter, named by the father only as he prepares to kill her (6.213), is Virginia. She must die, she is told, to uphold the family honour:

'Is ther no grace, is ther no remedye?'	*mercy*
'No, certes, deere doghter myn', quod he.	*my dear daughter said*

(6.236–7)

Figure 1 Virginius killing his daughter Virginia, *Roman de la Rose*, BL Harley 4425, fo. 54v. Roman historian Livy has Virginia stabbed; Chaucer adopts the preference of his immediate source, Jean de Meun, for beheading.

And so Virginia is decapitated. For no good reason, as it turns out: for had Virginius turned to the people for help, his daughter could have been saved. But no aristocrat, in this tale-world, would turn to the 'peple' (6.260), and so she dies. This is a horrible tale, not well told and rarely taught. When it *is* taught, students are revolted and incensed. So too, within the tale, is Harry Bailey, the Host, an innkeeper of Southwark. He reaches for closure, hoping to find some *sense* in this spectacle of a father holding his daughter's head by the hair: 'she was too beautiful to live' (6.293), pathetically, is the best he can do. This tale told by a medical doctor, he fears, is bringing on a heart attack (6.313). He needs medicine, he needs ale, he needs 'myrthe or japes' right away, if he is to be saved. He therefore commits himself, seeking bodily and spiritual salvation, to a professional teller of tales: the Pardoner. Nobody likes the feeling of being *trapped* in a film, flight, date, sermon, or business meeting that is apparently interminable, or just plain bad. Our medieval counterparts suffer extreme bodily symptoms in comparable situations. Madonna Oretta, in the first story of Boccaccio's *Decameron*, Sixth Day, is escorted by a gentleman who promises to tell her 'one of the best stories in the world'. But he butchers it, messing up every aspect of plotting, delivery, and style. Oretta sweats, has heart palpitations, and thinks she will die. She cannot simply *interrupt* this cack-handed cavalier, since this would cut at his manhood; she desperately needs a witty verbal formula. Fortunately, she finds one, and the situation is saved. Chaucer is similarly fascinated by physical reactions brought on by tale-telling, good and bad, inside and outside his tale-worlds. Roger the Cook experiences paroxysms of pleasure (compared to a good back scratch) as he listens to the *Reeve's Tale* (*CT* 1.4325–6); Criseyde, in Chaucer's great epic of ancient Troy, first considers falling in love on hearing a ravishing song (*T&C* 2.827–75). For a poet moving between court and city audiences, calculation of emotional reactions was a lifetime's study, and sometimes a matter of life and death. Skilled in artistic craft, Chaucer survived the turbulent reign of Richard II; the less-skilled Thomas Usk, a scrivener whose prose *Testament of Love* borrows from *T&C*, was beheaded, untidily, in 1388.

Persona

In distinguishing the first-person 'I' seen and heard within Chaucer's poems from the historical G. Chaucer, Esquire, royal servant, critics typically apply the term, to the first of these Chaucers, of *persona*. This perhaps derives from *Personae*, a collection of poems published by Ezra Pound in 1909. In pondering how a poetic 'I' might be distinguished from its poetic author, however, Pound was himself likely influenced by his reading of Chaucer. Both Pound and T.S. Eliot were avid readers of Dante, and here too distinctions are made between Dante the pilgrim or *personaggio* inside the text and Dante the author (*autore*) outside it. The 'I-Chaucer' or Chaucer *persona* found within Chaucerian fictions is a modest figure with, so he realizes, much to be modest about. The question 'What are *you* doing here?', put to him overtly in the dreamscape of *The House of Fame* (line 1883), resonates widely. In *The Parliament of Fowls*, which begins with galactic visions and ends with talking birds, the dreaming Chaucer cannot for the life of

7

him decide which of two contradictory gateway inscriptions applies to *him*. The choice seems crucial, since the opening of each translates directly from Dante's hell gate, 'Per me si va' (*Inferno* 3.1, 4, and 7; 'Thorgh me men gon', *PF* 127, 134). Finally his dream-guide, the Roman general Scipio Africanus the Younger, simply shoves him through the gateway, declaring that such inscriptions 'have nothing to do with you' ('nys nothyng ment bi the', 158). Having told Chaucer, bluntly, that he is no longer in the game as a lover, Scipio goes on to define the role that Chaucer *is* tasked to perform:

'But natheles, although that thow be dul,   *nonetheless not too bright*

Yit that thow canst nat *do*, yit mayst thow se.   *yet that which see*
For many a man that may not stonde a pul   *survive a throwdown*
Yet liketh hym at wrastlyng for to be,   *still enjoys*
And demen yit wher he do bet or he.   *and still judge whether he does better*

And if thow haddest connyng for t'endite,   *ability to write*
I shal the shewe mater of to wryte.   *things to write about*

(*PF* 162–8; emphasis added)

Many men who attend wrestling matches, and would be crippled by a single slam, nonetheless like going to the wrestling, making free with their opinions over who fights best. Chaucer is like this in matters of love: clueless himself, he can nonetheless pay attention and hence, if he knows how to write, compose poetry. And of course, he already has: the stanza of rhyme royal above, a verse form that Chaucer seems to have invented, is exquisite. Chaucer's modesty is

8

not, however, entirely formulaic. He knows that his English poetry, judged against French and Italian standards, lags several generations behind. And he knows that while he works *for* the court, he is not really *of* it. He is, at best, an adjunct or co-opted member of the royal household, working hard at its periphery—and not as a poet. Chaucer, the son of a London wine merchant who has received a good education, and has served in aristocratic households, has certainly gone up in the world. But not *very* far (Figure 2).

Figure 2 Pier Paolo Pasolini filmed *I Racconti di Canterbury* (1972) with himself as Chaucer, quill in hand. Like Chaucer, he is present both within and beyond his own fiction: inside as Chaucer *persona*, and outside as film-maker.

'Chaucer was a Class Traitor'

Terry Eagleton's whimsical *Ballad of English Literature*, sung to the tune of *Land of Hope and Glory*, a heady paean to imperialism composed by Edward Elgar and A.C. Benson in 1902, opens by proclaiming that

> Chaucer was a class traitor
> Shakespeare hated the mob

Eagleton goes on to condemn a panoply of English (and Irish) writers who fall short through various shades of political conservatism, conformism, and backsliding: only Milton, Blake, and Shelley are true revolutionaries. A germ of fact enables Eagleton's broad-stroking satire: Chaucer *did* move from one class to another. He was born (early 1340s) in Vintry Ward, a Thameside area favoured by wine importers such as John Chaucer, his father. John and his wife Agnes, niece of the 'moneyer' at the mint in the Tower of London, which loomed close by, procured good schooling for young Geoffrey at or close by St Paul's. They then placed him in a magnate (top aristocratic) household: that of Elizabeth de Burgh, Countess of Ulster. Magnate and royal women maintained separate households; young Geoffrey, likely still a page boy, first enters the historical record in April 1357 on being granted 'necessaries at Christmas', a gift of clothes and shoes ('chausseurs pour le Chaucier', might someone have joked?). Two years later, Chaucer followed Prince Lionel, Elizabeth's husband, into the English army, joined up with Lionel's father, Edward III, near Reims, where kings of France were crowned, and was promptly captured.

Ransomed for £16, a decent sum, Chaucer delivered letters back to London in October 1360 pertaining to the Treaty of Calais. Chaucer largely escapes the historical record during the ensuing years of truce. On 20 June 1367, however, he appears among annuitants in the royal household. It is because of his career-long royal service that Chaucer's life is well documented: much better than, say, Shakespeare's. He became what we would now term a civil servant. The most important appointment of his life, to last for twelve years, came on 8 June 1374, when Edward III made him controller, or chief tax inspector, of wool (England's most important export). This midlife return to childhood haunts on the north bank of the Thames was strange for Chaucer: born and bred among the London merchant class, he now came to inspect and tax them. What kind of *persona* might this royal appointee have fashioned to face the world while overseeing the Thameside quays? He seems to have made few friends.

European Theatres

Born in London, Chaucer died at Westminster sometime in October 1400. His burial place in the Abbey eventually became Poets' Corner, and admirers from the sixteenth to the twentieth centuries never tired of hailing him as 'the father of English poetry'. As such, it was reasoned, he must surely embody those qualities of Englishness most admired at the time of writing. In 1946, Marchette Chute published a book called *Geoffrey Chaucer of England*, as if our man is about to lead out the national football side for the first

11

post-war international friendly. All this is understandable, especially in the context of 1946, but quite wrong. Chaucer was first and foremost a European: if there were to be a heroic trio of European English writers, to match Eagleton's revolutionaries, my vote would go to Chaucer, Milton, and Eliot (George, rather than T.S.). Chaucer was hardly English at all: that is, his home base of operations was an area taking in the south-east quadrant of England, the Channel, which he crossed many times, and the English-controlled continental region bordered by Flanders, Artois, and Picardy. Since he seems never to have travelled in Scotland, Wales, Cornwall, Ireland, or England north of Yorkshire, he might more plausibly be known as 'Geoffrey Chaucer of Logres', the region south of the Trent, as demarcated by Geoffrey of Monmouth's *History of the Kings of Britain*. And also by Arthurian romance, although this would not have pleased Chaucer since, following contemporary Italian fashion, he regarded Arthuriana with amused, almost affectionate, contempt. He knew of Italian literary fashions because he had travelled in Italy, owned at least two Italian texts, and translated brilliantly from Italian (where modern translators stumble). French he knew as the most prestigious of English vernaculars, vital for life at court, diplomatic exchange, legal debate, pillow talk with his wife, and *badinage* with his sister-in-law, Katherine Swynford, *née* de Roet, mistress and later wife to John of Gaunt. Latin, beaten into him as a boy, was the language of the Church and Bible; Englishers of the Bible were criminalized during Chaucer's lifetime and, shortly after that, faced death by burning.

Chaucer, then, was no 'little Englander'. He understood many languages, and also how one language or dialect along any given route modulates into another—much as accents change between Bristol and Cardiff, or Philadelphia and Boston. He also heard tongues combining to form interlanguages, much as Scandinavians today pool their Norwegian, Swedish, Danish, and even Icelandic to fashion working idioms. His boyhood and then manhood on Thameside quays formed a perfect linguistic testing ground as goods from Francophone, Flemish, Dutch, 'Deutsch', and Italian locales were exchanged. From such poly-vocalities Chaucer fashioned his English. His choice to put all writerly eggs in one English basket remains remarkable: his friend and fellow poet John Gower, across the river at Southwark, chose otherwise, spreading himself between Latin, French, and English. But the English that Chaucer chose to write, one might say invent, opens out to Europe, rather than withdraws from it. His aim, a mere aspiration in *HF* but achieved by the end of *T&C*, is to make English illustrious by European standards *as* a European language. And strangely, in this regard, he showed the way to the future: for English really did become, at least before Brexit, the *patois*, the *lingua franca*, of all Europe. The notion of an un-European England would, for Chaucer, make no sense at all.

But is it archaic to speak of Europe, and European-consciousness, in this way? I would suggest not. Firstly, the standard T and O map of the Middle Ages, as derived from Isidore of Seville, divides the northern hemisphere into three, with Europe and Africa sharing the bottom and Asia

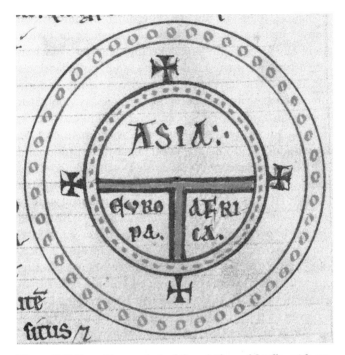

Figure 3 T-O world map, derived from Isidore of Seville, with settling places of Noah's sons Shem (Asia, on top), Japheth (Europe), and Ham (Africa).

(where the sun rises, and where Eden was) on top (Figure 3). Jerusalem sits dead centre, at the crossing of the T, and so Britain, as featured in more elaborate maps, lies on the periphery. The O represents the encircling ocean, and the

T the Mediterranean, the sea dividing or conjoining the three continents.

The heroine of Chaucer's *Man of Law's Tale*, an emperor's daughter called Custance, spends many years traversing the Mediterranean, sailing or drifting between Rome, Syria, Morocco, Gibraltar, Northumberland, and Rome. Her troubles begin when news of her outstanding virtues is carried by Syrian merchants, in a boat doubling as Cupid's wooden arrow, from Europe to Asia. Syria's sultan is seriously smitten, first by hearing of, and then imagining, this female paragon, acclaimed by the people of Rome as 'of al Europe the queene' (2.161). This sultan is a sympathetic figure. His mother is a pantomime villain, although her zeal keeps faith with her understanding of

> 'The hooly lawes of our Alkaron,
> Yeven by Goddes message Makomete.'   *given   messenger*
>   *Mohammed*
>
> (2.332–3)

The company of Syrian merchants in *The Man of Law's Tale* that does business in Rome is admired by one and all for being steadfast and true to its own values ('sadde and trewe', 2.135), and also for the quality of its spices, gold cloth, and coloured satins. Admiration for peoples of the three continents that shared the Mediterranean, and for their faiths, is not hard to find in the Middle Ages, or in Chaucer. In *HF*, for example, Chaucer sees a huge gathering of heralds tasked with celebrating the memory of great knights, all wearing the coats of arms

> Of famous folk that han ybeen   *have been*
> In Auffrike, Europe, and Asye,
> Syth first began the chevalrie.   *since   chivalry*
>
> (1338–40)

The idea that Africa, Europe, and Asia could pursue common ideals of chivalry is confirmed by the magnificent *Catalan Atlas* produced by the Jewish cartographers Abraham and Jafuda Cresques *c.*1375, and spirited away to the Louvre palace, Paris, soon after (Figure 4). This represents Saharan knights riding forth, on camels rather than horses, and kings with distinctive coats of arms (plus scimitars).

Salah ad-Din Yusuf ibn Ayyub, Syria's first sultan, was widely admired in the west even though (or perhaps because) he had crushed the Crusader army at Hattin, Palestine, in 1187, effectively ending Western hopes in the Holy Land. Saladin, as he was known in the West, is sighted in Dante's Limbo among virtuous pagans (*Inferno* 4.129), just before Aristotle; in Boccaccio's *Decameron*, he stars in two *novelle*, almost bookending the work (1.3 and 10.9). The occurrence of Jewish chivalry might seem less likely, but in fact, the scheme of the Nine Worthies, popular until the time of Shakespeare, features three Jewish knights keeping company with King Arthur, Emperor Charlemagne, and Godfrey of Bouillon (conqueror of Jerusalem in 1099), along with Alexander the Great, Hector of Troy, and Julius Caesar of Rome.

In spinning out the drama of Roman Custance as she sails between three continents, Chaucer emphasizes that she is an emperor's daughter, saying so not once, but three times:

Figure 4 Detail from *Catalan Atlas* made *c.*1375 by the map-makers from Mallorca, Abraham and Jafuda Cresques, featuring *Mansa Musa*, king of gold-rich Mali.

> Of the Emperoures doghter, dame Custance
> O Emperoures yonge doghter deere   *young dear*
> An Emperoures doghter stant allone   *stands*
>
> (2.151, 447, 655)

An emperor's daughter actually did stand at the heart of the court served by the mature Chaucer: Anne of Bohemia, daughter of Charles IV, Holy Roman Emperor. Arriving in England in late 1381, aged fifteen and with no dowry, Anne married Richard II on 20 January 1382. In milking pathos for a lonely 'Emperoures doghter', an epithet that also attaches itself to Griselde in the *Clerk's Tale* (4.168), Chaucer knows that such a one is not far away. Chaucer scripted arguments assiduously for the use of wives married to irascible men: if women such as Dame Prudence in *The Tale of Melibee* and Alceste in *The Prologue to the Legend of Good Women* cannot dissuade their men from vengeful violence, then blood will flow. Queen Anne, eight months older than her spouse, was comparably pacifying. When she died in 1394 (Figure 5),

Figure 5 Tomb of Richard II and Anne of Bohemia, Westminster Abbey, made after Anne's death but before Richard's by mason Henry Yevele (who had earlier worked under Chaucer). The gilt bronze effigies, by coppersmiths Nicholas Broker and Godfrey Prest, originally depicted the couple holding hands.

King Richard shed blood in the sanctuary, stabbing a courtier who came late to the funeral.

While alive, however, Anne represented not just a putative *protectrix* for errant courtiers, such as Chaucer, but also a conduit to a greater world. The magnificent Prague, built and ruled over by Anne's father, still viewable today from the Charles Bridge, was Europe's most sophisticated city. Charles IV, of the House of Luxembourg, was the first European monarch to write his own biography, in Latin, and he commanded many languages. Crossing the Alps in 1354, he met with Petrarch in Mantua before being crowned Holy Roman Emperor at Rome. Having changed his name from Wenceslaus to Charles by way of inviting comparisons with Charlemagne, crowned at Rome in 800, he went one better by importing Benedictines from Croatia to sing in Slavonic at a purpose-built monastery in Prague: he would be an emperor of east *and* west. Chaucer's Europe, then, extended very far from London and Westminster. This Europe was also, sad to say, a theatre of war.

Theatres of 'War! War!'

The conflict later known as the Hundred Years War began before Chaucer was born, and continued long after his death. The English were most famous for fighting, and continental Europeans were amazed at how good they were at it. Petrarch marvelled that *the English*, an unpedigreed people from the end of the world, should have captured King John II of France at the battle of Poitiers in 1356, and the nations of Europe were shocked by Agincourt in 1415. Chaucer, we have noted, fought briefly and ingloriously in France. The truce of which he carried news from Calais to Westminster in 1360 left thousands of English fighting men stranded: no troop ships waited to ferry them home. Many of them banded together, headed south, and terrorized the papacy at Avignon. Having been bought off, they crossed the Alps and served as *condottieri*, or mercenaries, to despots such as the Visconti at Milan and Pavia or republics such as Florence. The best of them, Sir John Hawkwood, himself inspired many literary tales, and was eventually memorialized by Paolo Uccello at the Florentine cathedral of Santa Maria del Fiore, riding an ambling charger (1436).

Chaucer, too, offers painted memorials to war—in the temple of Mars in his *Knight's Tale*. These lines far excel anything in Boccaccio's *Teseida*, his source (Italian has too many vowels for great war poetry). War, as Chaucer sees it here, is an unhappy aggregation of local crimes: pick-pocketing, burning stables, a nail through the skull, the suicide, 'The smylere with the knyf under the cloke' (1.1999). Presiding over all this is *Shit Happens* or *SNAFU*, as modern soldiers might call it; the sheer randomness that decrees that one person shall die, or be maimed, where another emerges unscratched:

Amyddes of the temple sat Meschaunce,	*in the middle* *Misfortune*
With disconfort and sory contenaunce.	*a miserable* *expression*
Yet saugh I Woodnesse, laughynge in his rage,	*Madness*
Armed Compleint, Outhees, and fiers Outrage;	*Quarrel Alarm fierce*

The careyne in the busk, with throte ycorve;   *corpse bush*
                                                throat slashed
A thousand slayn, and nat of qualm ystorve.   *not killed by plague*
The tiraunt, with the pray by force yraft;   *tyrant prey removed*
The toun destroyed, ther was no thyng laft.   *nothing left*

(1.2009–16)

Part of what is seen here are allegorical personifications: states of mind or being, such as Madness, externalized as if real persons. Other lines give us sharply-focused images, such as the corpse draped in a bush (our modern word *ambush* derives from such sneak attacks). Middle English poets, and supremely Chaucer's contemporary Langland, in his *Piers Plowman*, move between inner states of mind and sharp external imagining with a fluency not recaptured in English writing until modernism, from Virginia Woolf to Samuel Beckett. Modern editors, finding little punctuation to guide them in medieval manuscripts, often struggle: should 'disconfort' and 'sory contenaunce' be capitalized as boon companions of 'Meschaunce'? Or do they, as given above, attach adverbially to Mischance, indicating the unhappiness of his or her posture? Such uncertainties further fuel our unease in this shop of horrors, and there is more to come. Mars, we are told, is especially associated with

The barbour, and the bocher, and the smyth   *barber butcher*
                                              blacksmith

(1.2024)

Should that be *butcher* or *botcher*? A man tasked with removing a lance tip that has entered your eye and exited your ear might qualify on both counts. Barber-surgeons, whose bloody trade is still memorialized by red and white poles outside barber shops, might have little formal training. Their brief was to apply very quick fixes after battles. Small wonder, then, that the Temple of Mars depicts 'a thousand slain': not by the plague, but perhaps, in part, by butcher-surgeons.

And yet the minute we leave this Temple of Mars, recollection of war's horrors evaporates. People are thrilled by cavalcading, exotic knights, and Chaucer flatters the home crowd:

For if ther fille tomorwe swich a cas,	*occurred such an event*
Ye knowen wel that every lusty knyght That loveth paramours and hath his myght,	*who loves in courtly fashion*
Were it in Engelond or elleswhere, They wolde, hir thankes, wilnen to be ther– To fighte for a lady, benedicitcc! It were a lusty sighte for to see.	*if you please want Lord bless us! that would be*

(1.2110–15)

We thus pass rapidly from seeing in detail what war entails to total, flag-waving amnesia—as if transported back from the muddy trenches of the Somme to the late summer of 1914. Duke Theseus, who commissioned the war paintings, retains his inside knowledge—and so, in writing the poem, does Chaucer. He may not have fought for long, or at all, but he long served those who did. As Clerk of the King's Works, a job held for two years from July 1389, he arranged scaffold seating for noble and royal viewers of chivalric tournaments. Tasked with accommodating knights from England and overseas, and with sustaining enthusiasm for fighting, he was dogged by knowing what followed after—such as drinking herbal remedies in the hope of keeping a limb (1.2714). Such double consciousness typified his time. His *Tale of Melibee*, however, assigned by Chaucer the author to Chaucer the Canterbury pilgrim, debates how best to respond to an act of violent provocation. 'Yonge folk' leap to their feet, urge that iron be struck while still hot, 'and with loud voys they criden "Werre! Werre!"' (7.1036). An old man rises to counter them, delivering a meditation on *getting into war* that could scarcely be bettered:

> Lordynges...ther is ful many a man that crieth 'Werre, werre!' that woot [*knows*] ful litel what werre amounteth. Werre at his bigynnyng hath so greet an entryng and so large that every wight [*person*] may entre whan hym liketh and lightly [*easily*] fynde werre; but certes what *ende* that shal thereof bifalle, it is nat light to knowe. For soothly, whan that werre is ones [*once*] bigonne, ther is ful many a child unborn of his mooder [*mother*] that shal sterve yong [*die young*] by cause of thilke [*this*] werre, or elles lyve in sorwe [*sorrow*] and dye in wrecchednesse. And therfore, er that [*before*] any werre bigynne, men moste have greet [*great*] conseil and greet deliberacion.
>
> (7.1038–42; emphasis added)

The old man would say more, but is shouted down. War frames *CT* from beginning to end. Its first three pilgrim portraits are of professional fighters, seen just before the May campaigning season (and perhaps travelling on to Dover).

The Knight has campaigned and tourneyed across all three continents, at and well beyond the pale of Christendom. His son, the Squire, has fought more locally in territories bordering the English stronghold of Calais; he has taken part in 'chyvachie' (1.85), the scorched earth policy by which the English trashed French and Flemish countrysides, forcing terrified country people to hide in tunnels, as in Vietnam. The Knight's Yeoman is armed to the teeth, although his arrows and 'myghty bowe' (1.108) attract the most attention; it was longbowmen who gave the English army its real edge in battle, most famously in Agincourt's technological slaughter.

Many of Chaucer's travels, so inspiring for his poetry, were commissioned to further the war. He besieged Reims as Guillaume de Machaut, the greatest French poet and composer of the age, defended it. He might have learned about astrolabes and astrology during his 1366 journey to Spain, from Muslim-derived sources, but was likely briefed to help the Black Prince with troop movements. He visited Florence in 1373, just as Boccaccio was spearheading public interest in Dante, but his official business was with the Genoese, the chief shippers and hence troop transporters of the age. His 1378 trip to Milan, where Petrarch had lived for six years, was to recruit the tyrannical Bernabò Visconti and Sir John Hawkwood, now Bernabò's son-in-law, against the French. If Chaucer's theatre of literary operations was truly European, then, this Europe doubled as a theatre of war. Exotic visitors from the eastern Mediterranean, such as Levon V of Little Armenia and Philippe de Mézières, sometime chancellor of Cyprus, attempted to divert Anglo-French

Figure 6 Tomb of the Black Prince, Canterbury Cathedral.

hostilities into joint expeditions against Ottoman incursions. Prince Lionel, Chaucer's first master, tried to insulate the English in Ireland against Irish contamination in 1367, through the Statutes of Kilkenny. In 1399, Lionel's nephew, Richard II, was back in Ireland, protecting England's western flank; England was thus exposed to invasion by Henry Bolingbroke, Richard's cousin. The Brittany of Chaucer's *Franklin's Tale* was a Hundred Years War hotspot, and Chaucer's description of its rocky geography beats any French source. Consciousness of war thus accompanies Chaucer's pilgrims down the Canterbury road—which was also the road to Dover, and the Calais bridgehead. Had his pilgrims ever reached Canterbury, they might have visited not just the shrine of Thomas Becket, murdered by royal soldiers in 1170, but the tomb of the Black Prince, the greatest of English commanders, dead in 1376 at forty-five (Figure 6).

2

Schoolrooms, Science, Female Intuition

Chaucer's contemporary, Christine de Pisan, characterizes her own path to authorship as a 'road of long study' (*Le chemin de longue étude*, 1402–3). In his *Prioress's Tale*, Chaucer shows two schoolboys taking baby steps down this road in learning *grammatica*, or grammar. They are thus entering the educational scheme of the *trivium*, dedicated to grammar, rhetoric, and logic (or dialectics). Beyond this lie the higher arts of the *quadrivium* (arithmetic, geometry, astronomy, and music). *Trivium* arts were never to be seen as *trivial*, since they remained fundamental to all study, even at university. In the *Miller's Tale*, however, the Oxford student Nicholas, much given to singing and astrological divination, is impatient to move onto higher things. This 'poure scoler', we are told,

> Hadde lerned art, but al his fantasye   *the basic arts curriculum*
> Was turned for to lerne astrologye
>
> (1.3191–2)

Back in the 'litel scole' of the *Prioress's Tale*, ambitions are more modest—although its 'litel clergeon' protagonist is also, like Nicholas, anxious to rush ahead. His task is to 'syngen and to rede' (7.500), although he must sing before he reads, and sing before he knows what he is singing about. If he gets ahead of himself, neglecting his basic instructional 'prymer', he will be beaten, he says, three times an hour (7.542). Much violence attended scenes of instruction in the medieval schoolroom, where switches and canes lay always handy; there is a reason why we speak of academic *disciplines*. Undaunted, our hero finds himself strangely drawn to memorize a song called *Alma Redemptoris Mater*:

Noght wiste he what this Latyn was to seye,	*he didn't know meant*
For he so yonge and tendre was of age.	*because young*
But on a day his felawe gan he preye	*one day fellow student beg*
T'expounden hym this song in his langage,	*interpret in his own*
Or telle hym why this song was in usage;	*in use*
This preyde he hym to construe and declare	*begged construe*
Ful ofte tyme upon his knowes bare.	*bare knees*

(7.523–9)

His fellow schoolboy, slightly more advanced, tells him a little (the song is about the Virgin Mary) but no more:

'I kan namoore expounde in this mateere.	*can no more on*
I lerne song; I kan but smal grammeere'.	*know only a little*

(7.535–6)

His reluctance to say more stems from ignorance *and* awareness that saying too much, wading deeper into construing and expounding, can be dangerous. In the medieval schoolroom, and pulpit, interpreting was the privilege, jealously guarded, of clergy. The 'litel clergeon' will eventually master grammar, giving him access to what the text literally says. Only if he grows up to become a clergyman, however, will he be licensed to speak at higher levels of interpretation. Consider the story of Noah's ark—so central to the *Miller's Tale*, set in Oxford. Most everyone knows this tale, although confusion can reign even at the most basic, literal level (Box 1). Since old carpenter John remembers the tale but dimly, from 'ful yoore ago' (long ago, 1.3537), Nicholas the Oxford student can speak of Mrs Noah refusing to enter the boat, neatly conflating the Biblical account with that of popular ('mystery') plays. The second level of interpretation, in a fourfold schema, is the allegorical: what does that boat represent? Answer: the Church. The third and 'moral' level prompts the question 'what should I do, *quod agas*?' To which the answer here must be: get into that boat. The fourth level or sense of Scripture, known as the anagogical, asks what relevance this might have to the four last things (heaven and hell, death and judgement). Answer: if I get into that boat, I may be saved.

Devising and applying such higher interpretations was overwhelmingly the monopoly of men; women were generally classed (along with the 'litel clergeon') as literalists or 'fleshly' readers, unable to perceive higher, more spiritual levels of interpretation. And since the only Bible officially available was in Latin, women depended upon the work of male interpreters. Every woman in Chaucer's Oxbridge pairing of tales, those of the Miller and Reeve, is screwed (literally) by an Oxbridge undergraduate.

> **BOX 1** *A rhyme for remembering the fourfold method of interpretation*
>
> ··
>
> Litera gesta docet, quid credas allegoria,
> Moralis quid agas, quo tendas anagogia.
>
> The letter teaches events; allegory, what you should believe; morality, what you should do; anagogy, where you should aim.

Chaucer had himself studied into the far reaches of the *quadrivium*, the advanced range of topics associated with arithmetic, geometry, astronomy, and music. This led him to Boethius (*c.*480–524 CE), the sometime Roman senator whose Latin formed a major conduit for ancient Greek learning. Having been imprisoned at Ravenna by Theodoric, king of the Ostrogoths, Boethius composed his *Consolation of Philosophy* before being put to death. Chaucer, like so many after him in dangerous premodern times, was moved and inspired by the *Consolation*; Queen Elizabeth I, imprisoned in the Tower of London as a young princess, translated it as a mature woman. Chaucer's *Boece*, as his translation is known, stages a dialogue between Lady Philosophy and a dejected prisoner; hard lessons in prose, delivered by the Lady, are sweetened by alternating verses. The *Boece* represents Chaucer's most sustained engagement with *logica* or dialectic, the second science of the *trivium*, while also touching elevated philosophical subjects. It also shows Chaucer's determination to infuse English with philosophical heft or *gravitas*, so that more complex matters might be addressed *in English*. Which leads us back to the classroom, and Chaucer's *Treatise on the Astrolabe*. This guide to a scientific instrument, used to locate and predict planetary and solar positions, was written (Chaucer tells us) in response to the request of a promising, 10-year-old 'sone':

> Lyte Lowys my sone, I aperceyve wel by certeyne evydences thyn abilite to lerne sciences . . .

> (1.1–2)

Little Lewis seems, like the 'litel clergeoun', to be getting ahead of himself in the sequence of studies—but Chaucer is sympathetic to his cause. 'This tretis' or treatise, Chaucer says,

> . . . wol I shewe the under full light reules and naked wordes in Englissh, for Latyn canst thou yit but smale, my litel sone. But natheles suffise to the these trewe conclusions in Englissh as wel as sufficith to these noble clerkes Grekes thes same conclusions in Grek; and to Arabiens in Arabik; and to Jewes in Ebrew, and to Latyn folk in Latyn; which Latyn folk had hem first out of othere dyverse langages, and writen hem in her owne tunge, that is to seyn, in Latyn.

> (1.25–36)

> . . . will I present to you in very easy style and in unadorned words in English, for as yet you know small Latin, my little son. But nonetheless, let these true conclusions in English serve you as well as these same conclusions in Greek serve noble Greek scholars; and as Arabians are served by Arabic; and as Jews by Hebrew; and as Latin people by Latin. For these same Latin people first derived these conclusions from various other languages and wrote them in their own tongue, which is to say, in Latin.

Chaucer's commitment to 'Englishing' here shares common ground with arguments advanced in the Prologue to the Wycliffite Bible. If French, Bohemian (Czech), and other peoples have the Bible in their mother tongue, that Prologue reasons, why should not the English? This dissident religious movement associated with the Oxford theologian John Wyclif (c.1320–84), popularly known as Lollardy, had made Englishing the Bible a central demand (and accomplished activity). Lollardy, fashionable with some of Chaucer's acquaintances early in his career, turned perilous once Wyclif took on sacramental theology, specifically transubstantiation, thus tinkering with the holy of Catholic holies. It turned lethal with the accession of Henry IV in the last year of Chaucer's life; the statute *De heretico comburendo* ('on the burning of heretics') was rushed through in 1401. With remarkable prescience, Chaucer's *Astrolabe* grasps this gathering alliance between language and Crown, in effect giving us the very first conception of 'the king's English':

> And preie God save the king, that is lord of this langage, and alle that him feith berith and obeith, everich in his degre, the more and the lasse.

> (1.56–9)

> And pray that God may save the king, who is lord of this language, and all those who keep faith with him and obey him, each person according to his station in life, the greater and lesser.

But for the most part Chaucer avoids such dangerous issues— which grew rapidly more dangerous after his death—aided as ever by his hapless self-projection, his *persona*. In *HF*, he positions himself *authorially* as a scientist, eager to explore dream theory, the structure of the cosmos, the 'natural inclinations' of all things (734), the big bang theory ('he that mover is of al', 80), and the nature of thought (thinking here inevitably 'of Boece', 972). Yet his chief instructor is a talkative bird who drags him skyward in his claws, complaining that the roly-poly Chaucer has serious weight issues (574). One lesson concerns the nature of sound, 'soun':

'Soun ys noght but eyr ybroken;	*nothing but broken air*
And every speche that ys spoken,	
Lowd or pryvee, foul or fair,	*loudly or privately*
In his substaunce ys but air.	*is in substance nothing but air*

(765–8)

The 'natural inclination' of all speech is to move to the place where the House of Fame is to be found; and there, each speech reassumes the shape of the person that spoke it. This fantastical conceit, in a poem stuffed and buttressed with learned source citation, medieval footnoting, typifies a poem perched somewhere between science and farce, the cosmos and the body (with its sound-emitting orifices). And this is a place where Chaucer often, imaginatively, chooses to dwell. His *Summoner's Tale* concludes with a conundrum, pondered by three characters: how to divide a fart into twelve equal pieces? One remembers his science:

'The rumblynge of a fart, and every soun,	*sound*
Nis but of eir reverberacioun,	*is nothing but air*
And ever it wasteth litel and litel awey'.	*fades away bit by bit*

(3.2233–5)

But this speaker, a lord of the manor, finds no solution: 'it is an inpossible', he says (3.2231), the kind of university logical exercise known as an *impossibilium*. But his squire Jankyn reminds us that if, by this air-breaking theory, a fart *is* speech, then it may speak as commentary: that very day he had been moved to fart three times during a sermon. Jankyn goes on, like a good canon lawyer, to solve the problem by attending to nitty-gritty detail. Many manuscripts preface his triumph with a rubric:

> *The wordes of the lordes squier and his kervere* [carver of meat] *for the departynge of the fart on twelve.*

Chaucer is often celebrated for his bawdy, but this misses the point—or gets just half of it. Strange conjunctions of intellectual abstraction and bodily urges fascinate Chaucer—as later they would fascinate François Rabelais, Laurence Sterne, and James Joyce. Medieval medicine, for example, worked with calendars, charts, and scientific lore gleaned from Greek and Arab sources: but the sick body ultimately contracts to a channel between mouth and anus, susceptible to neither 'Vomyt upward, ne dounward laxatif' (*CT* 1.2756). Humans are unique amalgams of the animal and angelic, bodily impulse and pure intelligence. Dream theory, perennially fascinating for Chaucer, strives to know whether a specific dream is a message from above presaging the future, a *visio* or *oraculum*, or the after-effects of last night's dinner (red wine and rich cheese), or tangled bedclothes (*phantasma, insomnium*). And a *somnium* is yet trickier, requiring close interpretation. Animal fables, with talking birds or foxes, simply reflect and rejig our human

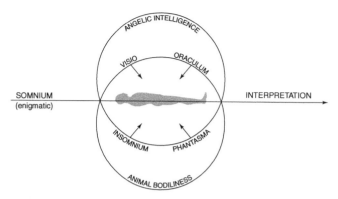

Figure 7 *Dreaming and the human condition.*

condition as intelligent animals. Sometimes, in bleaker moments, humans may envy the simplicity of animal life: for a beast, as the Theban knight Arcite says, may simply 'al his lust fulfille' (1.1318), not worrying about a life to come; but men suffer in this world, and then suffer again in the next (1.1315–24). Humans cannot aspire to live like angels, since that would be presumptuous, and to live like a beast is equally damnable. Walking the fine line of the human condition (Figure 7) is a perilous art; bawdy bodies and stargazing intelligences often misalign.

Female Learning, Women's Intuition

At the opening of her *Book of the City of Ladies*, Christine de Pizan despairs at being a woman. The great weight of texts written over centuries affirms women's lesser nature, and their inferiority to men. But such texts, Chaucer's Wife of Bath would say, are all men-penned:

By God, if wommen hadde writen stories,
As clerkes han withinne hire oratories,   *have in their chapels*

They wolde han writen of men moore wickednesse   *would have*
Than al the mark of Adam may redresse.   *race of men put right*

(3.693–6)

Few women at the time of Chaucer and Christine de Pizan learned to read and write; female counterparts to Chaucer's 'litel clergeoun' are hard to find. Some premodern women became scholars, painters, and bards because their fathers were: such is true for Christine, Artemisia Gentilleschi (1593–1653) and Gwerful Mechain (active 1462–1500; not in *ODNB*). Most women were forced to depend upon men to author and translate texts for them. Chaucer's Wife is often read as if she were a woman, but she is in fact a tissue of the anti-feminist texts (she trades in *textus*, cloth) that so depressed Christine: as men have said women are, so the Wife of Bath will be. The Wife is to Chaucer as Falstaff is to Shakespeare, a figure so compelling as to inspire spin-offs and guest appearances (in a poetic epistle sent to a man called Bukton, contemplating marriage; in the tales of the Merchant and Clerk). But Chaucer is not a woman, even while impersonating one, and he will not always honour the trust that women put in him. He says so himself, in effect, in his *Wife of Bath's Tale* (3.951–82). King Midas hides a secret from everybody but his wife, but she needs must blurt it out: 'Myn housbonde hath longe asses erys two!' For fuller details, says Chaucer by way of wrapping up the anecdote,

Redeth Ovyde, and ther ye may it leere.   *read   learn all about it*
(3.982)

Anyone capable of reading the Latin of Ovid's *Metamorphoses*, however, will find that it was Midas's barber, not his wife, who spilled the secret of his ass's ears. Trust that women *must* place in men as honest textual transmitters (being denied access to texts themselves) is here misplaced. The same thing happens again, yet more egregiously, in the *Nun's Priest's Tale*:

Mulier est hominis confusio–   *woman is man's ruin*
Madame, the sentence of this Latin is   *essence*
'Womman is mannes joye and al his blis'.
(7.3163–5)

Behind the patronizing speaker here (a cock addressing a hen) is an unnamed priest tasked to service the needs, textual and spiritual, of nuns. His tale revisits his boyhood world where, as a 'litel clergeon', he struggled to master rhetorical arts and read beast fabulists such as Aesop. He finds his fictional counterpart in Chauntecleer, the strutting cock, thus casting the nuns he serves as hens in a henhouse. In deliberately misconstruing Latin for 'madame', he masquerades or vogues as a grown-up *clergeon*, signalling to all other Latin-literate men above the heads of innocent, unlettered women. He is one more man not to be trusted.

Some women, however, did know Latin—and these include the Second Nun, one of those women served by the Nun's Priest and the very next tale-teller, according to the Ellesmere manuscript. Her tale of St Cecilia, a leader of men in early Christian Rome, presents itself as direct translation from Latin. Her story or *legenda* is prefaced by some fancy etymologizing of both Latin and English names (8.85–119). Here we find one woman, at least, speculating beyond the literal sense. Such skills would have been learned at the convent itself, since Latin was needed for singing the daily office. Convents in England, much thinner on the ground than in Germany or the Netherlands, educated young aristocrats and girls from the aspirational merchant class. The Anglo-Norman source text of Chaucer's *Man of Law's Tale*, by Dominican friar Nicholas Trevet, was written for Marie of Woodstock, a royal nun of Amesbury. Some convents boasted a pedigree, and traditions of distinguished Latinity, extending back to Anglo-Saxon times, and it is possible that Chaucer had a daughter or two at one or more of them. It is a strong bet, then, that the Second Nun sees what the Nun's Priest's mistranslating Chauntecleer is up to.

Medieval men were puzzled that, despite their monopolizing of texts, they were so routinely outdone in everyday verbal exchanges. A man might *see* what a woman is up to, but she can talk her way out of anything. Chaucer's *Merchant's Tale* actually mythologizes this state of affairs by inventing a neo-Ovidian fable. Pluto, king of the Fairies, sees a blind husband who is about to be cuckolded; his wife will climb on his back to meet her lover in a pear tree. Pluto resolves to restore the old man's sight. But Proserpyna, queen of the Fairies, decrees that the young wife and all women ever after will be gifted with 'suffisant answere':

> '...I shal yeven hire suffisant answere,   *give her*   *sufficient*
> And alle women after, for hir sake'.
>
> (4.2266–7)

Thus, while the old husband, January, certainly sees young May, his wife, fornicating up a pear tree ('and in he throng', 4.2353), May talks her way out of it. Which is only to be expected, says Rosalind in *As You Like It*, speaking of wifely wit, and continuing Chaucer's mythologization: 'You shall never take her without her answer, unless you take her without her tongue' (4.1.162–4). Respect for women's rapidity of thought is widespread in premodern, male-authored texts (such as Boccaccio's *Decameron*, especially in its Sixth and Seventh Days). The more recent notion of *women's intuition* upholds this notion of women thinking quickly and acutely beyond reason (where plodding, male-governed logic cannot follow). Pandarus, at a pressured moment of *T&C*, places all hopes in such peculiarly female ability: 'Wommen ben wise', he reminds his niece, Criseyde, 'in short avisement' (4.936). And, not long after, Criseyde affirms this talent by telling Troilus of her brilliant brainwave:

> 'I am a womman, as ful wel ye woot,   *as you know full well*
> And as I am avysed sodeynly,   *quickly inspired*
> So wol I telle yow, while it is hoot.   *will   hot off the press*
>
> (4.1261–3)

Such intuitive, inspired female thinking sometimes works and sometimes not; here it proves (at least for Troilus) disastrous. Such quick-fire cerebration can serve men, in tight situations, but they more generally fear it as something exceeding male networks of knowledge—which is to say, textual evidence, *auctoritee*. Such fears grow greater when men see women in groups, or especially when a younger woman keeps company with an older one. When Sir Gawain sees two women sitting together in Bertilak's castle, in *SGGK*, he is charmed by the younger and (privately) repulsed by the elder. He fails to see that the danger to his self-displaying moral perfection, his pentangle pride, lies in their *combination*; Morgan le Fay transmits female knowledge to the young wife. The Wife of Bath, similarly, learns trickery or 'soutiltee' from her mother, 'my dame' (3.576), to be passed on in turn to her well-loved niece (3.537). Her mother was her best teacher, the Wife says, having shared a husband-scamming anecdote:

'. . . I folwed ay my dames loore,	*always my mother's teaching*
As wel of this as of othere thynges moore'.	*in this as in many other matters*

(3.583–4)

Men, foolish creatures, put down everything they know in books—which may, as by the Wife, be radically edited, revised, or torn up. Female knowledge passes from woman to woman, beyond the ken of men. Of course, *The Wife of Bath's Tale* does *seem* to suggest that a young man, a knight-rapist, learns 'What thyng is it that wommen moost desiren'

(3.905). He at least has the brains to hit the road, rather than leaf through books. His winning answer is supplied by 'a wyf' (3.998, soon specified as 'an olde wyf', 3.1000) and delivered to an all-female parliament, representing the three conditions or *estates* of women (wives, virgins, and widows, 3.1025–6). It might be thought that this unnamed male simply takes the place of a younger woman (such as the woman he raped—now presumably neither virgin, wife, nor widow) to whom an 'olde wyf' would entrust her know-ledge. But does he now really *know* 'What thyng is it that wommen moost desiren'? The female parliament does not say so (although many readers assume that they do):

In al the court ne was ther wyf ne mayde,	*wife nor virgin*
Ne wydwe that contraried that he sayde,	*nor widow who contradicted*
But seyden he was worthy han his lyf.	*said deserved to live*

(3.1043–5)

A man who spends a year asking women questions, and listening to their answers, is a rarity (it seems) worth keep-ing. But there is no evidence that he knows what passes *between women*; that remains out of reach, like some distant fairyland. So it remains, it seems, for Chaucer. He has him-self commended, in *HF*, for his 'labour and devocion' to love (666), but he remains an outsider, a bug-eyed reader who simply replaces one book with another after a hard day at the customs house:

For when thy labour don al ys,	*day's work is done*
And hast mad alle thy rekenynges,	*you have balanced your books*
In stede of reste and newe thynges	*instead of rest and recreation*

Thou goost hom to thy hous anoon,	*you go straight home*
And, also domb as any stoon,	*as dumb as a stone*
Thou sittest at another book	
Tyl fully daswed ys thy look.	*dazed, befuddled*

(652–8)

Chaucer is sympathetic to women, depends upon their patronage and protection, imitates their voices, and tries to please them. But ultimately (and it is no small artistic achievement to express this), women are different. To say 'mysterious' is needlessly to exoticize; *different* simply suggests alternative ways of thinking, imagining, and being. As such, they excite his imagination—as do certain *differently* different men.

3
A Life in Poetry

Chaucer long aspires to *poetry*, but only on completing his great masterpiece of extended narrative, *T&C*, does he think he has achieved it. *HF*'s bookish musings suggest that he does indeed long to be associated with great poets such as Vergil and Ovid. But on being asked, while dream-touring the House of Fame, *what are you doing here?* ('what doost thou here than?', 1883) he finds no coherent answer. Earlier in that poem, the eagle carrying him heavenward had yelled 'wake up!' ('Awak') and then called him 'by my name' in a voice to be compared, Chaucer slyly suggests, with that of his wife (556–62). Pasolini makes much of this moment, as the dreaming Chaucer (played by the film-maker himself) is jolted from reverie by a shrill female voice offstage, calling his name: Chaucer-Pasolini must get to work, and make a living (see Figure 2). Chaucer's Francophone wife Philippa, who had married down, knew that no money, prestige, or preferment was to be had from writing English poetry. In fact, 'English poetry' was a contradiction in terms, since *poetrie* was ancient and *Englissh* barely born as a civilized medium; it is possible that Chaucer's wife never bothered to learn it.

In growing up on the Thameside quays, 'litel clergeoun' Chaucer, tasked to 'lerne song' (*CT* 7.536), had been surrounded by all kinds of ditties, stories, songs, traveller's tales, tolling of bells, barking of wares, and cries of the street: the stuff, in short, of modern urban poetry. The House of Rumour in *HF* strongly evokes urban noise, but the greatest muse of medieval London soundscape is William Langland, Chaucer's contemporary; the relationship of Chaucer to Langland (did they ever meet?) remains a great enigma. The Prologue to Langland's *Piers Plowman*, which rewards close comparison with *CT*'s *General Prologue*, ends or dissolves into a phantasmagoria of workaday sounds. Ditchdiggers sing as they work,

And dryveth forth the longe day with	*pass*
Dieu vous save Dame Emme!	*God save you*
Cokes and hire knaves cryden, 'Hote pies, hote!	*cooks boys hot*
Goode gees and grys! Go we dyne, go we!'	*suckling pig*
	let's go eat!
Taverners until hem tolden the same:	*said the same to*
	them
'Whit wyn of Oseye and wyn of Gascoigne,	*white wine*
	Alsace
Of the Ryn and of the Rochel, the roost to defie!'	*Rhine*
	la Rochelle wash
	down the roast!
—Al this I seigh slepyng, and sevene sythes more.	*saw seven*
	times as much

(B 225–31)

Oxford of the *Miller's Tale* is similarly noisy. Between Nicholas's singing of the *Angelus ad virginem* near the beginning

(1.3216) and his bum-scalded yell near the end (1.3815), we have Absolon fiddling and singing a high treble, the pre-dawn ringing of a church bell, the singing of friars, a fart, a spell, a cock crow, and Alison's citation of a pop song ('com pa me', 1.3709). Such Bedlam would not have impressed Philippa Chaucer, whose proper place was not London, but Westminster, or wherever else her life took her as demoiselle of her namesake and compatriot queen. Nor, so far as we know, did it inspire Chaucer's earliest composing—although he does, at the very end of *CT*, admit to writing 'many a song and many a lecherous lay' (10.1087). Embracing the social amplitude of London would come later for Chaucer; he made his start by, so to speak, following in his wife's footsteps.

But we should not turn so abruptly away from the alternative English literary tradition represented by *Piers Plowman*, even if Chaucer's Parson, the last of the Canterbury tale-tellers, quickly disavows it:

> But trusteth wel, I am a Southren man: *a Southerner*
> I kan nat geeste 'rum, ram, ruf', by lettre.   *tale-tell*
>
> (10.42–3)

The verbal phrase 'I kan nat' here, as elsewhere in Chaucer, means not simply 'I cannot', but rather 'I lack the technical ability to . . .' (from *koude*); as a Southerner, the Parson *could not* master such a verse form. But he does recognize it: the succession of three alliterating consonants here precisely pinpoints the pattern of the standard line (aa/ax, with the *caesura* or midline pause observed and the final consonant *not* alliterated). And although this is a northern or more

45

properly north-western poetic tradition—which might help explain how a Cheshire household utterly defeats an effete southern visitor in *SGGK*—there was plenty of opportunity to hear alliterative poetry in London, and perhaps also in Westminster (Richard II had a strong Cheshire powerbase). *St Erkenwald*, set at St Paul's Cathedral, sees a bishop's involuntary teardrop serving to baptize an ancient pagan, unearthed during building work (see p. 92). *St Erkenwald*'s sophisticated layering of human histories is matched by *The Siege of Jerusalem*, an alliterative poem owing much to the 'Ebrayk Josephus' found bearing up 'the fame of . . . Jewerye' in *HF* (1433–6). Alliterative poetry, with its clashing and crunching consonants, is especially good at sieges and battles. When Chaucer comes to describe the battle of Actium in his 'Legend of Cleopatra', a tale made famous by 'Hebrew Josephus', he drifts into alliterative style (*LGW* 635–48). He does so again as the key battle of the *Knight's Tale* grows climactic:

In goon the speres ful sadly in arrest;	*spears go firmly into the lance-holder*
In gooth the sharpe spore into the syde.	*spur into the horse's flank*
Ther seen men who kan juste and who kan ryde;	*knows how to joust*
Ther shyveren shaftes upon sheeldes thikke.	*shafts shatter upon thick shields*

(1.2602–5)

Clearly, some line of continuity connects such passages with the great battle poetry of Anglo-Saxon England; quite how it runs continues to baffle scholars. When we speak of Chaucer 'aspiring to poetry', then, we must remember that Anglo-Saxon England had already generated a language fit not only for great poetry, such as *Beowulf,* but for the kind of administrative, legal, and historiographical tasks that, in Chaucer's lifetime, were entrusted chiefly to Latin. We should also note that Chaucer's alliterating contemporaries in no way shrank from absorbing French influences. Bertilak's castle in *SGGK* is equipped with highly fashionable, chalk-white chimneys (*chymnees,* from French, 798) and *Cleanness,* another of the four poems in the great British Library manuscript, Cotton Nero A.x, refers us to Jean de Meun's continuation of the *Roman de la Rose.* The fact that we are referred to the '*clene* Rose' (1057, emphasis added) is, as we shall shortly see, knowingly ironic.

French Lessons

It was once thought that Chaucer's creative career developed from a French phase, through Italian, to a final triumph of English; the notion of a later London 'homecoming' lends tacit support. But Chaucer never stopped learning from Francophone poets, and never stopped speaking French. The most extensive first-person statement we have from Chaucer is actually in the French of England, or Anglo-Norman. This forms part a lengthy court case of 1386, a matter of honour between two knights found to be sporting the same heraldic coat of arms. Hundreds testified—including Owain Glyndŵr, who had recently been fighting for Richard II against the Scots. French was the undisputed language of chivalry, as its

47

etymology (from *cheval*, horse) implies; the Black Prince, Chaucerian England's greatest hero, was remembered through Chandos Herald's verse life in Anglo-Norman. It is of fundamental importance to grasp that 'nationality' at this time was not simply equated with the language you spoke. When Henry V ordered a new warship, he named it *Grace Dieu*; when men spoke of 'the English nation' in Ireland they thought primarily of aristocratic families linked by birth (*natare*, to be born) rather than state apparatus. When Italian despots such as the Visconti wanted to relax, they read French romances. When distinguished poets such as the Savoyard Oton de Granson (much admired by Chaucer) came to fight for the English, he carried on writing in French. When the poet-historian Jean Froissart joined the household of Queen Philippa of Hainault (and of the future Philippa Chaucer), he persisted with French, even when chronicling English triumphs in the Hundred Years War. And in traversing the theatre of that war, young Chaucer encountered many poets dedicated to the arts of the *dit*, the *rondeau*, and the *ballade*. One of them, Eustache Deschamps, earlier burned out of his home by an English raiding party, or 'chyvachie' (*CT* 1.85), mock-commends Chaucer for being a 'great translator' of French, and for planting '*la Rose*' in English soil.

Chaucer very likely tried translating the *Rose* into English early on; at least one Fragment (A) of the surviving *Romaunt of the Rose* translations suggests his poetic DNA. The *Rose*, surviving in some 320 manuscripts, a staggering number, is medieval Europe's most influential poetic text. Its first part, composed by Guillaume de Loris *c.*1230, is a delicate allegory (Figure 8), featuring a trip to the pool of Narcissus in the Garden of Love, and encounters with aspects of the lady's psyche (*Bel Acueil*, Encouraging Welcome; *Daunger*, Holding Back). It ends with the lady, figured as a rosebud, trapped in a tower. Forty years later, the poem is taken up by Jean de Meun, translator of Boethius (cribbed by Chaucer) and of the Heloise and Abelard letter exchange. The latter, like much else from medieval Paris, feeds into Jean's massive extending of the *Rose* from 4059 to 21258 lines, and is picked up by the Wife of Bath (herself part-composed from *Rose* materials), who speaks of 'Helowys / That was abbesse nat fer fro Parys' (3.677–8). The extended *Rose* ends with an assault on the tower imprisoning the lady, and then on the lady, that turns poundingly pornographic. Christine de Pizan, just a year after Chaucer's death, objected and then quarrelled by letter with Jean Gerson, Chancellor of the University of Paris, inspiring *La querelle de la Rose*.

Chaucer, inveterate borrower and pillager of poetic material, took liberally from the *Rose*—not only for his Alisoun (Wife of Bath) and his Virginia (*Physician's Tale*), but also for 'madame Eglentyne', his Prioress. But the French poet he most warmed to was Guillaume de Machaut (*c.*1300–77), the greatest poet-composer of the age. Machaut was comfortably installed as a canon of Reims cathedral, the coronation place of French kings, long before Chaucer came to besiege the city in 1359. They may have met afterwards, at Calais in 1360, but Chaucer was in any case a lifelong admirer and part of Machaut's international, courtly nexus. Pierre de Lusignan, King Peter of Cyprus, was royally entertained by Edward III in

Figure 8 Lover entering the garden, *Roman de la Rose*, Netherlands, c. 1490–1500, BL Harley 4425, fo. 12v. He is led by the figure of Oiseuse, 'Idleness'; only those with time on their hands may enter this garden.

1363 and had many English followers. In 1364, he attended King Charles V's coronation at Reims (a busy day for Machaut); Peter's own cathedral at Famagusta, where the Lusignans had themselves crowned kings of Jerusalem, was modelled on Reims. In 1365, Peter 'conquered' (not for long) Alexandria, and was the toast of Western Christendom: Froissart chronicled the triumph, and Machaut began his *Prise d'Alexandrie*. However, on 17 January 1369, Peter was assassinated by his own knights. Chaucer, borrowing more from Machaut's 'Conquest of Alexandria' than from eye-witnesses, has his Monk apostrophize 'worthy Petro, kyng of Cipre' (7.2391), fallen so far so fast. Chaucer's eight-line stanza ends with commonplaces ('Thus kan Fortune...' 8.2396), but coping with egregious twists of fate was one of the chief challenges for court-inspired poets. One strategy was posing questions about who suffers most: a lady whose lover is dead, or a knight whose lady proves faithless? Machaut posits one answer in his *Jugement du roi de Behaigne* [*Bohemia*], but has this reversed on appeal in his *Jugement du roi de Navarre*, a poem set in the catastrophic plague year of 1349. Chaucer learned much from these 'Judgement' poems and adopted the posing of 'questions of love': 'Yow loveres axe [*ask*] I now this questioun', says the Knight (1.347); 'Which was the moste fre, as thynketh yow?' asks the Franklin (5.1622).

Guillaume de Machaut was both a first-rate poet and a very great musical composer. His *Messe de Notre Dame*, still frequently performed and available in many fine recordings, is among the most exquisite of polyphonic masses. Machaut collected some 283 lyrics, some set to music and some not, in carefully organized 'complete works' manuscripts. And he experimented with placing musically-set lyrics within longer narratives, most appealingly in his *Voir Dit*, or 'True Poem'. Written when Machaut was in his sixties, this tells of the precarious love affair between an aging *artiste* and an ambitious, very young woman called 'Toute Belle' ('Totally Cute'). Toute Belle, keen to begin an artistic exchange, sends along her own compositions for musical settings and procures his original texts; the poet, totally smitten, worries that his work will be misconceived, or go astray. Toute Belle partly resembles Nynveh in Malory's *Morte Darthur*, the lady of the lake who drains all knowledge from Merlin, the love-besotted magician, before leaving him trapped beneath a rock. Toute Belle likely represents little beyond the ageing poet's neuroses. The poet-composer continues to be susceptible to beauty, including that of his own art, but fears waning and decay—much like Thomas Mann in Venice, gazing at the beautiful youth Tadzio in 1911.

Machaut fashioned a poetic persona suggesting that he is still in the game (of love); Chaucer, au contraire, suggests that he was never really in it. Chaucer further concedes that Chaucer, the poet-persona, is not too bright: a posture that works brilliantly for him in *The Book of the Duchess*, an early dream vision that leans very heavily on French, especially Machaut. The occasion is serious: on 12 September 1368, Blanche, Duchess of Lancaster, dies of the plague like her sister and father before her. Her father was Henry of Grosmont, co-founder of the Order of the Garter, first Duke of Lancaster, and author of the *Livre de seyntz medicines* (Book of Holy Medicines, a devotional treatise in Anglo-Norman). Her bereaved spouse is John of Gaunt, the most powerful magnate of the realm. A young commoner like Chaucer could hardly step forward to commiserate. But at some point, he did set to composing his *Book of the Duchess*. Within a dream, and in the context of a hunt, the Chaucerian first-person 'I' comes across 'a man in blak' (445), sitting with his back to an oak tree. This man composes a poetic 'compleynte', which he does not set to music (we are explicitly told, 471), but simply recites. Chaucer merely 'reherses' or sets down the eleven-line lyric, suggesting (and here following a Machaut strategy) that the best part of his poem simply transcribes original composition by the noble patron. The dreamer notes that this pale-faced knight has so 'argued with his own thoght' that 'he had wel nygh lost his mynde' (504, 511). Eventually, the knight notices the dreamer and addresses him (the dreamer is thrilled to note) as if he were somebody (530). Pressed to tell what ails him, the black knight explains that Fortune has played a game of chess with him—and taken his queen (654). Too dim-witted to understand this metaphorically, the dreamer asks for details of this 'los' (1302). Eventually, the grieving knight, still pressed by the dimwit dreamer, must speak the literal truth:

'Allas, sir, how? What may that be?'	*how (have you lost so much)?*
'She ys ded!' 'Nay!' 'Yis, by my trouthe!'	*is dead*
'Is *that* youre los? Be God, it is routhe!'	*that's a huge pity*
And with that word ryght anon	*immediately*
They gan to strake forth; al was doon,	*sound the horn for going home*
For that tyme, the hert-huntynge.	*the hunt of the he[a]rt*

(1308–13; emphasis added)

Chaucer's very obtuseness, or that of his dreaming 'I', here enables, within the standard octosyllabic couplets of French tradition, the first talking cure in English verse.

Italian Poetry and 'Drasty' English Rhyming

At some point during his Italian travels, in the 1370s, Chaucer fully grasped what Dante was attempting in his *Commedia*: to be guided into poetry, and exploration of the afterlife, by Vergil, the greatest of classical poets—and eventually, on both counts, to surpass him. Chaucer's *House of Fame*, composed like Dante's *sacro poema* in three parts, has been talked of as parodying the *Commedia*. But it is better understood as parodying itself: English 'poetry', when held up against the great Italian precedent, as driven to paroxysms of self-conscious embarrassment. Book I, which namechecks Dante at line 450, 'imitates' Dante by 'following' Vergil:

> 'I wol now synge, yif I kan,   *if I am capable*
> The armes and also the man'
>
> (143–4)

The 'yif I kan' here, breaking with Vergil's *Aeneid* to find a rhyme, means (as noted) 'if I am technically capable'; the answer given here must be 'not yet'. The eagle that swoops to lift Chaucer to the heavens in Book II is borrowed from Dante's middle cantica (*Purgatorio* 9.28–30), although no Dantean guide proves so tediously talkative. The opening of Chaucer's Book III lifts directly from the opening of Dante's Book III (*Paradiso* 1.13–27), but with modifications: Chaucer denies any ambition to show off 'art poetical', laments the failings of his verse, and promises Apollo (if things go well) to go kiss the nearest laurel tree; Dante, like Napoleon at Notre Dame de Paris in 1804, will crown *himself* with laurel. In approaching the House of Fame, Chaucer sees a series of niches *outside* the building, containing 'alle maner of mynstralles / and gestiours' (minstrels and tale-tellers, 1197–8). Chaucer feared that, however lofty his ambitions, his poetry might be taken as mere minstrelsy, given lack of English precedent. This anxiety is aired in *Sir Thopas*, the tale assigned in *CT* to the pilgrim Chaucer himself:

'Do come', he seyde, 'myn mynstrales,	*said my minstrels*
And gestours for to tellen tales,	*tale-tellers*
Anon in myn armynge,	*at once as I am armed*
Of romances that been roiales,	*royal*
Of popes and of cardinales,	
And eek of love-likynge'.	*also love affairs*

(7.845–50)

This 'drasty rhymyng' (shitty rhyming) is interrupted by the Host for being 'not worth a toord' (*turd*, 7.930). The pilgrim Chaucer defends it as 'the beste rhyme I kan' (7.928), and he has a point: these are the cards that English 'rhyme' has dealt him; half of all English romances surviving from this period are tail-rhyme. If he is to do better, then, and to stake a place for himself *inside* the House of Fame, he has far to travel.

It is worth noting, however, that much as John Mandeville overshoots Jerusalem in his *Book of Marvels and Travels*, so Chaucer wanders beyond the House of Fame to a whirling house of twigs, the domain of shipmen, pilgrims, and pardoners (2121–7). This suggests that even in contemplating a place on a plinth in Fame's House (and it has been suggested that the 'English Geoffrey' of line 1470 *may* be Chaucer, recognized for services to Troy), Chaucer is already contemplating a wilder and looser construction: a *Canterbury Tales*. Here his chief inspiration will be Boccaccio, the author from whom he borrows more than anyone else, but never names.

Italian Liberation, Rhyme Royal, and the Path to *Troilus and Criseyde*

Chaucer's admiration for Italian poetics inspired him to acquire manuscripts of two poems by Boccaccio: the *Teseida delle nozze d'Emilia* (*Theseus-Epic about Emily's Wedding*, chief source of the *Knight's Tale*) and *Il Filostrato* (*The Love-Struck Man*, source of *T&C*). Manuscripts were expensive: Chaucer might have done the copying himself, perhaps during the ample downtime of his 1370s Italian trips. Boccaccio copied out Dante's *Commedia* several times, for money and for personal use, and copying is of course the best way to soak up a text. The verse form of these two Boccaccian poems, written in the Francophone ambit of Angevin Naples, is *ottava rima*, an eight-line stanza of eleven-syllable lines rhyming *abababcc*. *Ottava rima* likely originated as a street-singing, popular form, but Boccaccio was the first seriously to apply it to epic events of Troy and Thebes. The form later became the great workhorse of Italian epic tradition, from Poliziano and Boiardo to Ariosto and Tasso; English adopters include Thomas Heywood (*Troia Britanica*), Aemilia Lanyer (*Salve Deus Rex Judaeorum*), and W.B. Yeats ('Sailing to Byzantium'). Chaucer clearly experimented for some years:

his *Anelida and Arcite*, marking early engagement with the *Teseida*, tries out a wide range of stanzaic forms; his *Complaint to his Lady* flirts with Dantean *terza rima*. But finally, he settled on a form he seems to have invented: rhyme royal. This seven-line stanza, rhyming *ababbcc*, was also to enjoy a distinguished afterlife, ranging from King James I of Scotland (*The Kingis Quair*) and Sir Thomas Wyatt ('They flee from me') to Shakespeare (*The Rape of Lucrece*) and, again, W.B. Yeats ('A Bronze Head').

Italian proved liberatory for Chaucer, not just because its hendecasyllabic (eleven syllable) lines allow more poetic elbow room than French octosyllabics, but because its metrics lie much closer to English. Where French lines, relying on syllable count, skim lightly, Italian is more *stressed* and em*phat*ic; Italian, like English looking back to Anglo-Saxon poetics, employs a caesura—generally with two stressed syllables before the midline division, and two after: 'Nel *mezzo* del ca*min* || di *nos*tra *vi*ta' (*Inferno* 1.1). Dante, whose most famous opening has just been cited, moves more deliberately than Boccaccio—whose lines frequently enjamb (run across line endings) to suggest *cursus*, a form of rhythmical prose he learned as a student, and that will flower into the great prose of the *Decameron*. Chaucer, in the very first stanza of his rhyme royal *Parliament of Fowls*, shows mastery of both options: slow and stately movement in the first three lines, and then mercurial, line-crossing movement in the last four:

| The lyf so short, the craft so long to lerne, | *life* | *learn* |
| Th'assay so hard, so sharp the conquerynge, | *attempt* | *painful* |

The dredful joye alwey that slit so yerne:	*fearful happiness slides away so fast*
Al this mene I by Love, that my felynge	*speak of in relation to consciousness*
Astonyeth with his wonderful werkynge	*is so sorely astonished by*
So sore, iwis, that whan I on hym thynke	*in truth think of Him (Love)*
Nat wot I wel wher that I flete or synke.	*I don't really know whether I float*

(1–7)

Chaucer opens here, like Dante following Vergil, by translating Latin: *ars longa, vita brevis*, art ('craft') takes so long to learn, and life is short. We might assume that *art*, specifically the writing of poetry, is Chaucer's subject here, but the last four lines, in the manner of a gloss, set us straight: what the poetic 'I' has in mind here ('mene' falling somewhere between the modern German *meinen* and the modern English *mean*) is Love. This 'Love' is to be identified with 'Cupide, oure lord' (212), a terrifying feudal figure who is not to be confused with cutesy Renaissance *putti*, or cherubs. Anyone struck by medieval Love's arrow experiences total disorientation, astonishment, not knowing whether they are waving or drowning.

This brilliant opening inducts us into a brilliant poem that covers vast territory in fewer than 700 lines. Beginning with speculation on dreams, on the cosmos, and the end of time (68–70), we pass through a Dantean gate (127–40) to a Boccaccian Temple of Venus, imitated from the *Teseida*. Uncomfortable at visions of Priapus, 'with hys sceptre in honde' (256), and of half-naked Venus, the dreaming Chaucer gratefully returns to the open air. Here he encounters a gathering of birds convened by Nature on 'Seynt Valentynes day' (386). Chaucer is generally credited with popularizing celebrations of St Valentine's Day, along with Oton de Granson, the Savoyard poet acknowledged by Chaucer's *Complaint of Venus* as 'flour of hem that make in France' (82). The concluding of Chaucer's bird parliament is celebrated by the singing of 'a roundel' (675), a French lyric form with a recurring refrain: 'The note' or tune, Chaucer says, 'imaked was in Fraunce' (677). Chaucer thus keeps faith with French poetics, and especially Francophone music, even in absorbing new Italian materials. But he also lets in English voices, from up and down the social register: water-foul, seed-foul, worm-foul, and up to the heights of magnate birds of prey. The Commons had begun separating from the House of Lords during the reign of Edward III, and Chaucer himself sat in the lower chamber in 1386 as one of two MPs representing Kent. Commons debate bred boisterous English, as some of the lines spoken in Chaucer's *parlement* suggest:

'Now fy, cherl!' quod the gentil tercelet,	*peasant noble male falcon*
'Out of the donghil cam that word ful right!'	*right out of the dunghill*

(596–7)

But the lower order birds find no difficulty in pairing off; it is the aristocratic lovers who hold up, so to speak, the process of Nature. A female eagle, courted by three noble lovers, asks firstly for more time (a year) and secondly for her freedom of choice to be respected (647–53). *Delay* is what makes courtly love distinctive (as opposed to Nicholas's grabbing Alisoun 'by the haunchebones', 1.3279), artistically productive (a space for lyric poetry), and frustrating—which brings us to *T&C*.

It is not obvious why Troilus needs to delay so long before contacting Criseyde: he is a bachelor prince, she is a widow, and no obstacle—beyond a gulf in social class—impedes their union. But perhaps expressing such a thought puts me among the worm-eaters. One must recognize that love, or subjection to medieval Love, is a terrifying business for men and women—not alike, but in different ways. A woman, mindful that she must guard her reputation, may find a lover's pleas for mercy coercive ('I will die unless you give in'). A man, fearful that he *will* suffer the torments of the damned if refused, may delay asking the question.

4

Poetry at Last

Troilus and Criseyde

Boccaccio wrote the *Filostrato* at Naples in his early twenties. Its Preface claims that the young, love-struck author's lady has moved away, beyond the mountains; this fits nicely with imaginings of Troy, with Greeks encamped beyond the city walls. Benoît de Sainte-Maure's *Roman de Troie* (*c.*1155–60) and its condensed Latin translation, Guido delle Colonne's *Historia destructionis Troiae* (1287), were the earliest texts to focus upon Criseyde's *amours*, providing relief from the steady diet of battles and truces. Boccaccio drew Criseyde much further into the foreground, focusing upon her relationship with Troilus. Things go well so long as the affair keeps within the walls of Troy; things go badly once politics dictate Criseyde's being given over to the Greeks in a prisoner exchange. Since London styled itself 'Troynovant' or 'New Troy', imagining itself founded by the Trojan-Latin Brutus, Chaucer immediately saw great potential in Boccaccio's *ottava rima* tale. London and Westminster, in Chaucer's time, were not the same place: London, protected to the east by the Tower of London (and by the Thames, and a city wall) was separate from the abbey and palace of Westminster. Between them lay open ground and Charing Cross, home to the Pardoner in his 'alien priory' of St Mary, Rouncesval (named after the mother house in Navarre, and the mountain pass where, according to the *Chanson de Roland*, Saracens massacred Christians).

Chaucer's walled Troy conflates city and palace. His imagining of a city besieged was fed by memory of 1381, when a peasant army had camped outside London and then poured in through Aldgate—the gate above which Chaucer, a royal servant, was then living (Figure 9). The mob sacked the Savoy palace of John of Gaunt, a Chaucer patron, murdered the Archbishop of Canterbury, and chased Flemings through the streets, 'shrille' for the 'kille' (*CT* 7.3395–6). Chaucer's *Troilus and Criseyde*, defined as a 'tragedye' (5.1786), tells of a doomed love affair in a doomed city. For three-fifths of its length, its trajectory is seemingly comic, or upward-moving. But this, Chaucer's Monk elsewhere explains, is part of tragic structure, since a tragic protagonist will enjoy 'greet prosperitee' before ending 'wrecchedly' (*CT* 7.1975–7); to wish somebody a tragic beginning and a comic end is to wish them continuous happiness. *T&C* Book III ends blissfully, but a turn of the page to Book IV (one of the most painful turns in all poetry) spells immediate, irrevocable disaster:

> And Troilus in lust and in quiete   *delight and tranquility*
> Is with Criseyde, his owen herte swete.   *own sweetheart*
>
> (3.1819–20)

Figure 9 Structure marking the location of Aldgate, by StudioWeave (2012), inspired by Chaucer's writing of *HF* and *PF*.

But al to litel, weylawey the whyle,	*too short a time, alas*
Lasteth swich joie, ythonked be Fortune	*does such joy last, thanks*
	to Fortune

(4.1–2)

When his love affair goes well, young pagan Troilus strives to connect personal happiness in love with the energy driving the cosmos, anticipating (and often echoing) Dante; when things turn sour, Chaucer leans increasingly on Boethius—but without hope of Christian consolation. Things complicate further as Trojans trapped in Troy read recreationally of Thebes—another doomed city. When Pandarus, pursuing Troilus's suit, comes to his niece Criseyde at the beginning of Book II, he finds her 'withinne a paved parlour' listening to 'a geste / Of the siege of Thebes'; what she knows in 'romaunce' form, he knows through Latin, the 'bookes twelve' of the *Thebaid* by Statius (2.82–108). Diomede, the Greek who will seduce Criseyde, has serious Theban lineage—and just as the soothsayer Cassandra is trying to tell her brother Troilus this, the *Thebaid*'s Latin argument comes crashing onto the page (in almost all manuscripts). Even Pandarus's first visit to Criseyde is framed with literary allusions portending no good. He is woken up that morning by the swallow Procne ('the swalowe Proigne'), who twitters about her transformation from woman to bird ('whi she forshapen was'); her sister Philomela has been abducted by her husband, Tereus (2.64–70). Later on in Book II, once she has learned of Troilus's love for her, Criseyde is lulled to sleep by a bird, singing perhaps 'in his briddes wise a lay / Of love' (2.921–2). She then dreams of another bird ripping out her

64

heart: an eagle, clearly to be identified as the royal Troilus (2.925-31). But the first, lulling bird was 'a nyghtyngale' (2.918), Philomela, Procne's sister. Tereus tore out Philomela's tongue once he had raped her; the liquid song of her transformed state, as a nightingale, speaks also to a bloody and violent past.

Such dense allusiveness suggests that with *T&C* Chaucer is writing a poem to be pondered over, many times, rather than listened to once. And it further suggests that, given history's tendency to run to ruin, in contexts of recurrent plague and war, moments of pure delight are especially to be treasured. Music, for Chaucer, seems optimal for such moments. Troilus falls in love because he is love-struck by the sight of Criseyde; his *innamoramento* seems as fatedly immediate as that of Ted Hughes on seeing Sylvia Plath (see the section 'Poetry, finally' in Chapter 7). Criseyde, however, does not fall in love in this way, but is made amenable to it through song. Her niece Antigone—the Theban name is worrisome, granted, and we are still in the first half of Book II—sings a song composed by a noble, female Trojan (2.827-75). Criseyde hears and *digests* this song slowly (2.899-903), and her resistance to love lessens ('she wex somwhat able to converte'). This seven-stanza song could have been sung in live performances of *Troilus*—of the kind imagined by the gorgeous frontispiece to the Corpus Christi, Cambridge, manuscript (MS 61). At any event, the song's chief source of inspiration is, inevitably, Machaut. One might at this point formulate a working hypothesis for Chaucerian inspiration: Italy for poetry, France for music. When he comes to embed a Petrarchan sonnet into Book I of *T&C*—the first and only English translation of a sonnet by 'the lauriat poete' (*CT* 4.31) before the sixteenth century, and a great prize—Chaucer devotes three stanzas to it. Two stanzas of rhyme royal, fourteen lines, could precisely have accommodated a fourteen-line sonnet. But since we have here a *song* of Troilus, a *Canticus Troili*, Chaucer stretches out to three stanzas—the standard length of a French *ballade*.

Chaucer does not appear as a character in *T&C*—this is not a dream poem, and it is set in ancient Troy—but still makes himself busy as *persona*. Early on, he again positions himself as an amatory no-hoper, mere servant of the servants of the God of Love (1.15): a celibate pope of poetry? It is as author of the very text he is producing that he will loom largest. Granted, at the beginning of Book II he says that he is merely translating 'out of Latyn', and that 'as myn auctor seyde, so sey I' (2.14–18). But the opening of this second book shows high ambition by resolutely imitating the open-ing of *Purgatorio*, Dante's second *cantica*, before delivering a statement on historical and cultural relativism that comes straight out of Dante's *Convivio*, Book I:

Ye knowe ek that in forme of speche is chaunge	*also*
Withinne a thousand yeer, and wordes tho	*then*
That hadden pris, now wonder nyce and straunge	*were valued foolish*
Us thinketh hem, and yet thei spak hem so,	*we think them*
And spedde as wel in love as men now do;	*got on as well in love*
Ek for to wynnen love in sondry ages,	*and also different periods of history*
In sondry londes, sondry ben usages.	*different countries customs differ*

(2.22–8)

It is poignant for us to contemplate this passage, over seven hundred years later: what Chaucer here posits about changes in forms of speech has come true, separating him from us. According to one popular misunderstanding of the Middle Ages, medieval people failed to grasp that customs change with time: why do people in medieval paintings of Nativities and Crucifixions stand around in medieval clothes? (But then why, one might ask, does painter Stanley Spencer in 1924–7 stage the Resurrection at Cookham, Surrey, in modern dress?) Chaucer concedes that such time-gulfs open, but proposes that they can be bridged. More remarkable, however, is his precise coordination of 'sondry ages' with 'sondry londes': just as we can empathize with persons living in distant periods of history, so we can come to understand those living in faraway countries. This marriage of cultural relativism with human empathy is something we still struggle to achieve.

Chaucer begins Book III of *T&C* with seven stanzas of authorial song: that is, he combines part of a song sung by Boccaccio's Troiolo with touches of Boethius and Dante to celebrate the universal sway of Venus; he then invokes Calliope, muse of epic poetry (3.45), and picks up the narrative action. But after Book III, as things run rapidly downhill, we increasingly encounter a poet at war with his own material: one of the strangest displays by an authorial *persona* in all literature. Chaucer now detaches himself from his own poem by speaking of what '*the storie* telleth us' (5.1037; 5.1051, emphasis added), and by refusing to endorse what 'men say' about Criseyde—namely, that she has abandoned Trojan Troilus for Greek Diomede:

Men seyn—I not—that she yaf hym hire herte.   *gave him her heart*
(5.1050)

The 'I not' here might mean 'I do not', but more likely means 'I don't know' (I ne woot, from *wissen*). Chaucer *persona* now seeks deniability not just for his story's outcome, but also for his newly-hatching reputation as a besmircher of women. This posture serves nicely to launch a new project: a *Legend of Good Women*, to be compiled as penance for the rest of his life, at express command of the God of Love, and to be presented to 'the quene . . . at Eltham or at Sheene' (F 496–7, specifications scrubbed from the manuscript once Queen Anne died in 1394). Chaucer *ipse* knows, however, that he has finally achieved something great with *T&C*: a work of poetry. The poem is to be sent to John ('moral') Gower, across the water at Southwark, and to 'philosophical [Ralph] Strode', Oxford don and/or London lawyer (5.1856–7). Future copyists of 'Troylus' will be enjoined to write 'trewe' (*Chaucers Wordes unto Adam, His Owne Scriveyn*), on pain of 'the scalle' (scaly scalp eruptions, 2–4). Such injunction is actually built into the fabric of *T&C*, where Chaucer, addressing his poem, prays God that 'non myswrite the' or 'the mysmetre (5.1795–6, *mis-metre thee*). Foreseeing wide dispersion of his poem, in time and space, Chaucer hopes that it will always be understood, whether read or sung (5.1797–8). This last proviso, 'or elles songe', again holds open the possibility that Chaucer, like Machaut, envisions lyric parts of his composition actually being *sung*. Or it could be that Chaucer is aligning himself with those opening lines of Vergil, so badly botched in *HF*: 'Arma virumque cano' (*Aeneid* 1.1; *HF* 143–4). Either way, some alignment with Vergil is clearly on his mind as he finally sends out his poem, instructing it not to get above itself,

But subgit be to alle poesye;	*but observe the pro-prieties of all poetry*
And kis the steppes where as thow seest pace	*you see walking before you*
Virgile, Ovide, Omer, Lucan, and Stace.	*Homer, Lucan, and Statius*

(5.1790–2)

Finally, Chaucer uses the p-word, obliquely suggesting that *T&C*, and hence its author (still a mere 'makere', 5.1787), might worthily walk behind great, antique poets: Vergil, Ovid, Homer, Lucan, and Statius. This notion of one modern joining a company of five classic poets borrows from *Inferno* IV, where 'la bella scuola' gathers around Vergil, and Dante finds himself honoured as 'sesto tra cotanto senno' (*sixth among such geniuses*, 4.94–102). Jean de Meun used this trope before Dante, and Boccaccio after him, so for Chaucer to pin such a bauble on his own poem suggests high estimation of his own poetic achievement, at a European level. It is debatable whether anybody else in England could recognize this badge of European honour, and in any event, such pretensions come crashing to earth in the *General Prologue* to *CT*:

Ther was also a REVE, and a MILLERE,	*Reeve*
A SOMNOUR, and a PARDONER also,	*Summoner*
A MAUNCIPLE and myself—ther wer namo.	*there were no more*

(1.542)

Here we find Chaucer, at the tail end of the pilgrim portraits, among low-life predators, swindlers, and word merchants, listed sixth of six. The Host, a Southwark innkeeper, will later look at Chaucer the 'popet' pilgrim and ask 'What man artow?' (7.695, 'what are *you* good for?'). The answer '*poesye* on a European scale, worthy of the ancients' would butter no parsnips. The only person travelling to Canterbury in search of a 'sixth' is the Wife of Bath: 'Welcome the sixte, whan that evere he shal' (*whenever he turns up*, 3.45). Chaucer, a widower, stands in need of a wife, and the Wife of Bath clearly becomes his vernacular muse. Geoffrey Chaucer, once *CT* is complete, becomes the Wife of Bath's sixth husband.

5

Organizing, Disorganizing

The Canterbury Tales

The chief precedent for *CT* as a framed collection is the *Decameron*, heroically written in response to the 1348 plague, but then retouched by Boccaccio until his death in 1375. Chaucer heard much about Boccaccio during his visit to Florence in 1373, the year of the world's first *lecturae Dantis* (Dante lectures, organized and given by Boccaccio). People think Chaucer mean never to have namechecked Boccaccio, since he took more from him than from any other writer, in any language. But when Chaucer makes reference in *CT* to Dante (3.1126, 5.1520, 7.2461) and Petrarch (4.31, 4.1147, 7.2325), he cites them as what we might now call *author functions*, detached from any concern with personality. Boccaccio, for Chaucer, was too much like himself: a personable poet, given to low-life *and* lofty concerns, following after Titans. Chaucer editors since the 1860s have suggested further alignment with Boccaccio by speaking of *CT* as a poem of ten 'Fragments', or tale-units, thus neatly matching the *Deca-meron*'s ten days (Box 2). This scheme, following the tale order of the famous Ellesmere manuscript, and reproduced in *The Riverside Chaucer*, provides a convenient scheme of reference (used earlier in this paragraph, and throughout this book). But its tidiness belies the messy and varied state of the fifty-five manuscripts where we find the *Tales* complete, or nearly so. Tale orders vary, and 'fragments' float. Rather than bogging down here in technicalities, we might just register the greater point that Chaucer, as compared to neatnik, completionist Boccaccio, was not much interested in finalizing his *CT*. For him, the framed collection provided a convenient workshop and repository for all kinds of writing, some of it drafted much earlier. And where Boccaccio homogenizes his sources into sausage-like production of one hundred prose *novelle*, Chaucer lets genre and literary form run wild. Such formal promiscuity suggests forms of challenge to social order not to be found in Boccaccio, or Shakespeare.

The original scheme of tale-telling proposed by the Host at Southwark begins unravelling from the start. His notion that each pilgrim should each tell two tales on the way to Canterbury, and then two on the way back, would generate more than a *Decameron*'s worth of stories, and with the Knight setting the pace at 1125 couplets, we would be in for more than 70,000 lines of verse. Fragment I does not so much end as dribble away as we enter a London whorehouse: 'Of this cokes [*Cook's*] tale' says the Hengwrt manuscript, Ellesmere's closest authoritative rival, 'maked Chaucer na moore'. In twenty-five *CT* manuscripts, not the most authoritative, the incomplete

BOX 2 *'Fragment' Order in* The Canterbury Tales, *following the Ellesmere Manuscript:*

··

    I: General Prologue
       Knight's Tale
       Miller's Prologue & Tale
       Reeve's Prologue & Tale
       Cook's Prologue & Tale

   II: Man of Law's Prologue, Tale, and Epilogue

 III: Wife of Bath's Prologue & Tale
       Friar's Prologue & Tale
       Summoner's Tale

 IV: Clerk's Prologue & Tale
       Merchant's Prologue, Tale, and Epilogue

  V: Squire's Prologue & Tale
       Franklin's Prologue & Tale

 VI: Physician's Tale
       Pardoner's Prologue & Tale

VII: Shipman's Tale
       Prioress's Prologue & Tale
       Prologue & Tale of Sir Thopas; The Tale of Melibee
       Monk's Prologue & Tale
       Nun's Priest's Prologue, Tale, and Epilogue

VIII: Second Nun's Prologue & Tale
       Canon's Yeoman's Prologue & Tale

 IX: Manciple's Prologue & Tale

  X: Parson's Prologue & Tale
       Chaucer's Retractions

Cook's Tale is followed by *The Tale of Gamelyn*. This sees a disinherited younger son take to the forest, embrace outlawry (but not women), and beat up clerics. Perhaps Chaucer had intended to rework this ballad-like romance into *CT*; perhaps *Gamelyn* was added by someone seeking to supply the Cook with a tale. Whatever the case, readers of these twenty-five manuscripts would have experienced Fragment I quite differently. *Gamelyn* bookends the opening tale of the landholding Knight most suggestively, while its Robin Hood-like forest exile and outlawry looks forward to *As You Like It*. Fragment II, a stand-alone performance of the Man of Law, 'floats' elsewhere in some manuscripts and puzzles with his suggestion that 'I speke in prose' (2.96: he speaks in rhyme royal). Had he originally been assigned the prose *Tale of Melibee*, derived from Albertano da Brescia, an Italian Man of Law, and finally palmed off to the pilgrim Chaucer? The Wife of Bath, beginning Fragment III, is the first pilgrim who just starts talking (rather than being asked, by the Host, to take her turn). Might she originally have been assigned what is now the *Shipman's Tale*, which starts off the ragbag Fragment VII? The teller of this tale muses on the sad plight of him who must pay for parties, dances, and fashion expenses, namely

The sely housbonde, algate he moot paye,	*poor always must*
He moot us clothe, and he moot us arraye,	*must dress us up*
Al for his owne worshipe richely,	*for his own social prestige*
In which array we daunce jolily.	

(7.11–14)

While we might have here a partnered-up Shipman who likes dancing in dresses, it seems likelier that his tale of wifely and clerical deceit in the mercantile world was first written for the Wife of Bath (before she got ideas of her own) and then offloaded on him, imperfectly revised. These and other examples suggest that Chaucer cared little about the final state of *CT*, or did not live long enough to care, in the way he so evidently did about *T&C*.

Despite such untidiness, amazing things happen in *CT*, beginning with the Knight. His tale of ancient Theban love reworks Boccaccio's *Teseida*, twin text to his *Filostrato*, but with great discipline. Boccaccio designed his *Teseida*, in twelve books, to be as long as Vergil's *Aeneid* (9896 lines). Chaucer's *Tale*, less than one quarter as long, conveys the *impression* (but not substance) of epic length through style. *Occultatio* (telling you something while saying that you are *not* going to talk about it) is a favourite trope here, with monumental non-descriptions of a feast (1.2197–206) and funeral (1.2919–66); when the Knight's son, the Squire, tries out this trope (5.63–75; 5.283–90), or any other trope, things fall apart. One *actual* textual cut acknowledged early on, however, cost Chaucer dear, namely the war between 'the regne of Femenye' and Theseus, the 'grete bataille' between 'Atthenes and Amazones', the besieging and then wedding of Hippolita (1.875–85). The wittily-gendered warfare of the *Teseida*'s first two books is delightful, but Chaucer 'moot as now forbere' (*must forgo it for now*, 1.885). The self-control shown in darkening and abbreviating Boccaccio's poem argues that Chaucer, of the baggy *CT*, *could* exercise artistic discipline when he really wanted to.

The Knight's Tale as a saga of ancient knightly love suggests strong continuity with Chaucer's earlier output, especially *T&C*. Clearly, the Host intends to follow an order of tale-telling that moves gently down the social order, from top to bottom. He had fixed things (so everybody suspects) to ensure that the Knight won the straw-drawing competition as first storyteller, and he had then turned to 'my lady Prioress' (1.837–9). Now, once the Knight is done, he turns to 'sir Monk' (1.3118). The Miller will have none of it,

But in Pilates voys he gan to crie,	*Pontius Pilate's voice began*
And swoor, 'By armes, and by blood and bones,	*swore by (God's) arms*
I kan a noble tale for the nones,	*know how to tell occasion*
With which I wol now quite the Knyghtes tale'.	*match*

(1.3125–7)

This is the revolutionary moment of *CT*, its point of no return. The drunken Miller cries like Pilate, a plum ranting part in the street drama tradition that informs his tale. Swearing fierce, physical oaths, he promises to 'quite' the 'noble storie' (1.3111) just heard with a 'noble tale' (1.3127). 'To quite' a tale can mean something as genteel as 'to requite' it—which is what the Host had in mind on turning to the Monk (1.3119). But as adapted by the Miller, and then by angry pilgrims such as the Friar and Summoner, it shades towards meaning 'get even with' (following some perceived social slight). The Miller's performance grounds or undresses the *Knight's Tale*'s lofty pretensions while *quiting* or upholding its logic: in matters of love, two into one won't go. It brings us from the ancient, classical, epical, geographically distant world ruled over by 'the grete Theseus', likened to 'a god in trone' (*a god on his throne*, 1.2529), to *now*, close to home, among people we know. Its epistemology is not that of philosophy, but of the body: the Miller *knows* he is drunk, he says, because sounds emitting from his mouth enter his ear and, yes, he can conclude, 'I am dronke' (1.3138). From cakehole to earhole; his tale will be full of holes.

This Miller, as described in his *GP* portrait, is armed and dangerous (1.545–66). The miller in the *Reeve's Tale* to follow is armed to the teeth, with a sharp sword at his belt, a dagger in his pocket, and a Sheffield knife in his hose (1.3929–33); 'no man dare lay hand on him' (we hardly need be told, 1.3937). Millers, fiercely proud peasants who were keen to preserve 'greet sokene' (1.3987), powerful local monopolizing of their grinding services, figured prominently among the rebels who had stormed and then occupied London in 1381. *GP*'s Miller, a decade later, defers to no man (1.3168), and the Host must manage him carefully. The Miller's winning argument for speaking out of turn, so to speak, is quite simple: 'I *wol* speke or elles go my wey' (1.3133, emphasis added). The Host clearly does not want the Miller to 'go his own way', and so tells him to 'tel on' (1.3134). The Host and his pilgrim 'compaignye' (1.24) work extraordinarily hard from first to last at keeping together, preserving integrity *as* a group; *compaignye*, from French, etymologizes as 'those who eat of the same bread'. Through their experience of trade, parish, and cathedral guilds all members of the pilgrimage know how to behave collectively; they also know how to seal a deal, such as that of the tale-telling regimen, with an oath and the drinking of wine

(1.810–21). Professional fights and squabbles along the way are resolved, as in guilds, through strenuous intervention. When a mysterious newcomer shows up just five miles from Canterbury, wishing 'To riden in this myrie compaignye' (8.586), the group repels him as a fraudster. And when, just two miles from Canterbury, the drunken Cook falls from his horse, the entire pilgrimage stops to hoist him back into the saddle again (9.46–55). And yet, despite such sustained attention to collective well-being, to arriving complete as a group, the very end of *CT* sees us suddenly divided into sheep and goats, with Chaucer praying 'that I may be oon of hem at the day of doom that shulle be saved' (*one of them that shall be saved on Judgement Day*, 10.1092). Resolution of this paradoxical conflict between all-for-one, collective action and apprehensive self-concern ('will *I* be saved?') must be laid at the door of the Church, or in the corner of Westminster Abbey, where Chaucer lies buried.

Genre: No Genre

Sixteenth-century editors of Chaucer needed to represent him as at once strange and familiar, foreign and one of us. He is one of us as an Englishman, and as founding father of a great poetic tradition. He is strange because Roman Catholic, on the far and wrong side of the Reformation. Emphasizing the strangeness of Chaucer's language helped to articulate this divide, and kept print editors gainfully employed in supplying glosses, commentaries, and textual apparatuses for their readership. We live with this legacy today: Chaucer is read aloud, when read at all, as medieval, in need of explaining, whereas Shakespeare performs as if contemporary, *de nos jours*. This arbitrary divide narrows if we follow Shakespeareans in aiming, above all, to *put over* the meaning of a passage; Chaucer can be performed by and through whole bodies, rather than declaimed from the page. One aspect of Chaucer did, however, genuinely baffle the sixteenth century: his wild variety of generic forms; his bewildering array of discursive performances *within* each form. Since Chaucer seems to have produced no single, stabilized, standardized literary form, the Boccaccian *novella* seemed a much better bet for adoption and imitation. Renaissance homogenization thus won out over medieval diversity.

Chaucer does provide some suggestions concerning form as guide to content, most notably with rhyme royal. Within *CT*, such stanzas as employed by the Man of Law, Clerk, Prioress, and Second Nun support serious, religiously inflected content. But Chaucer's longer-line, five-stress couplets, *CT*'s great metrical warhorse, support all kinds of narrative; Fragment I moves seamlessly downhill from Knight to Cook without a change of metre. Tail rhyme, a staple of popular Middle English romancing, features in the pilgrim Chaucer's *Sir Thopas* but is then chased from the stage by Chaucer's Host (7.919–31). The Host also abets the Knight in terminating the Monk's *ababccbc* stanzas (similar to, but not identical with, Boccaccian *ottave*), finding in them 'ne disport ne game' (*neither pastime nor fun*, 7.2791). The Monk's sin against conviviality lies not in narrating 'tragedie', his announced genre (7.1991), but one bloody tragedy after another, a catalogue of great men's falls.

The tale's manuscript subtitle, *De casibus virorum illustrium*, exactly reproduces the title of a Latin work by Boccaccio, a neo-humanist compiling of the fates of great men. It was under Petrarch's influence that Boccaccio turned away from vernacular (mother tongue) composition in the 1350s to concentrate on Latin encyclopaedism; another of his works, *De mulieribus claris*, supplied material for Chaucer's *Legend of Good Women*. In the *Monk's Tale*, Chaucer provides us both with a first English sampling of this proto-humanist genre and a first popular English reaction to it: boring!

Chaucer's Host also itches to interrupt the Squire, since the young man (the only person on pilgrimage known to be young) is floundering, unable to manage the elaborate figures of speech that his father, the Knight, has handled peerlessly. This time, it is the Franklin who drops the boom, with the Host following in close behind. His strategy, brilliantly simple, is pretending to assume that the Squire has finished storytelling (although he has, in fact, just sketched a fictional scenario that would detain us way beyond Canterbury): 'In feith, Squier, thow hast thee wel yquit' (*'Well done, Squire!'* 5.673). The Squire botches every fancy figure of speech attempted; his Sleep personified (5.347–56) is especially ludicrous. But what *genre* of tale is he telling? To say 'romance' again suggests kinship with his father, but qualifiers must immediately be added: classical romance (Knight) versus exotic or oriental romance (Squire)? But the Knight exoticizes intensively with paired descriptions of Thracian and Indian kings (1.2128–82), with thoughts of 'Femenye' and 'Scithia', beyond the European pale, and with general evocation of places far distant *in time*. Attempts to define the genre of any given Chaucerian tale soon founder, or pile up compound adjectives like *Hamlet*'s Polonius ('Tragicall-Comicall-Historicall-Pastorall', 2.2.399–400). Critical tradition once proposed that each Chaucerian tale expresses the unique character of its pilgrim (as described in *GP*) speaker. This has some merit for some pilgrims—considered as social types, rather than as unique persons. Most anarchic of the tale-tellers is the Merchant: his three pairs of protagonists are two months of the year (January and May), the King and Queen of the Fairies, and two Latin tags (court advisors Placebo, *I will please*, and Justinus, *the just one*—who makes learned reference to what the 'Wyf of Bathe' has recently said 'in litel space', 4.1687). Traditional social or *estates* theory, distinguishing between 'worshippers, warriors, and workers' (Figure 10), could not accommodate merchants, since they flourished by trading *between* social strata. *Piers Plowman*'s momentous pardon from Truth finds room for merchants only 'in the margyn' (B 7.18). Are merchants then to be seen as tradesmen-knights of the waves (*merchant venturers*, in a fifteenth-century formulation)? It is not surprising that mercantile self-representation fails to gel or stabilize in *CT*. Generic *bricolage*, as offered by *CT*'s pilgrim Merchant, perhaps faithfully conveys contemporary mercantile mimesis. Not all tales, however, match up so neatly with pilgrim portraits, and some tellers (Second Nun, Nun's Priest, Canon's Yeoman, Chaucer himself) have no *GP* portraits at all.

It is best to read any given tale, then, not with a priori notions of what its genre might be, but with genre as an open question. Generic conformity today has rigidified.

Figure 10 Capital C with cleric debating knight; peasant looks on. French, late thirteenth century, BL Sloane 2435, fo. 85.

Popular music is chopped up into subgenres to serve the needs of *niche* radio stations (although each artist, so defined, dreams of a *crossover*). When crocodiles surround Roger Moore in *Live and Let Die* (1973), the eighth Bond film, we know he is sure to escape without losing a leg, or loosening his tie; a Sam Peckinpah movie from the same period, or *Game of Thrones* from ours, would be messier. We know what to expect. But very often protagonists in Chaucer have no idea what kind of tale-world they inhabit. We, as readers, are equally uncertain, but much pleasure is to be had in finding out. The *Franklin's Tale*, for example, begins where most romances end: two young lovers plight their troths. The tale dedicates itself to exploring what happens *after* that moment ('have heer my trouthe', 5.759), and things go badly: another pledge of *trouthe* made rashly means that the young wife, Dorigen, must submit to sex with a man she hardly knows. Dorigen, in a long meditation, tries to think her way into a new genre. Many ancient noble women before her have preferred suicide to shame, so she will simply embrace this *legend of good women* and extend the list. Yet even as she tries to talk herself into this genre, she talks herself out of it, realizing *that's not me*. Finally, she does return to the romance world, where she and her husband live happily ever after ('in sovereyn blisse', 5.1552). But the *Franklin's Tale* is not yet over for other characters (the would-be lover, the magician). The closure it attempts to enforce by asking 'who behaved best' (5.1622) rings hollow, not least in excluding the tale's protagonist—Dorigen.

Chaucer's tales, then, typically defeat fixed notions of genre by performing themselves into existence, by finding out through narration what they are all about. It is no accident that returns from applying genre theory to Chaucer have been meagre, but for gender theory very great: Judith Butler's *Gender Trouble* handily beats out anything by H.R. Jauss. Chaucer's greatest performers, often considered as a pair, are the Wife of Bath and the Pardoner. Both in a sense are made of nothing, or, in the Wife's case, of a tissue of anti-feminist commonplaces; yet both, *while speaking*, seem compellingly real. Both are powerfully sexualized, the Wife by her own discourse and the Pardoner by the fascination others have with what lies 'in his lappe' (1.686). 'I trowe he were a geldyng or a mare' ('I *believe him to be* a castrated male horse, or a female horse', 1.691), says Chaucer, but he does not *know*; the Host late on proposes cutting off testicles that may or may not be there (6.951–5). The Pardoner's own rationales for living ring hollow: I want to take *everything* from the poorest widow in a village, he says, even if her children starve from famine; I want 'a joly wenche in every toun' (6.448–53). But he seems truly alive while performing, and drawing attention to, his own *techne*, his pulpit technique:

Thanne peyne I me to strecche forth the nekke,	*take pains to stretch*
And est and west upon the peple I bekke,	*I nod over the people*
As dooth a dowve sittynge on a berne.	*like a dove sitting on a barn*
Myne handes and my tonge goon so yerne	*move so rapidly*
That it is joye to se my bisynesse.	*to see me do my business*

(6.395–9)

Such coordination of neck, hand, and tongue movements, coupled with empty signifiers (fake relics, pardons), mesmerizes audiences even as they glimpse the fakery; the Host breaks the spell only through a crude counter-performance of imagined sexual violence. The contemporary performance form that comes closest to *Pardoner's Tale* is *vogue*, a highly stylized dance style that developed in Harlem before being mainstreamed by Madonna, and later by the famous 'walk off' in *Zoolander*. Voguing involves much attitudinizing and emphatic pointing, but not pointing *at* anything; attention fixates on the signifier (the finger; neck, hand, and tongue). There is no signified. Which brings us back to the Pardoner, who, it has been proposed, is a nihilist, a damned soul, a figure of despair: the projection, in short, of things most feared in medieval, and later, worlds. Contemporary gender and queer theory, however, sees social identity as performed and re-performed into being. The Pardoner does what 'we' do, but differently. No need to fear or cast off the Pardoner, then; he too is finding his way to Canterbury.

6

Something to Believe In

Chaucer's prayer to the Virgin Mary, called in manuscripts 'La priere de Nostre Dame' and today referred to as an *ABC*, unfolds through a series of eight-line stanzas, each beginning with a different letter of the alphabet. Here is the first:

Almighty and al merciable queene,	
To whom that al this world fleeth for socour,	*flees*
To have relees of sinne, of sorwe, and teene,	*forgiveness from trouble*
Glorious virgine, of alle floures flour,	*flower of flowers*
To thee I flee, confounded in errour.	
Help and releeve, thou mighti debonayre,	*relieve gracious (one)*
Have mercy on my perilous langour.	*languishing*
Venquisshed me hath my cruel adversaire.	*vanquished*

(1–8)

Chaucer is here translating from the French Cistercian Guillaume de Deguileville, who spent his life in a monastery north of Paris. Chaucer's *ABC* proved extremely popular, surviving in sixteen manuscripts, often accompanied by elaborate ornamentation. When English translators of Deguileville's lengthy *Pèlerinage de la Vie Humaine* (Pilgrimage of Human Life) came to the part from which Chaucer had sourced his *ABC*, they simply stopped translating themselves and dropped in Chaucer's poem. They could appreciate the skill with which Chaucer had expanded the monk's (standard French) octosyllabics into a longer, more capacious English line; and how he had reduced the line count of each stanza from twelve, in the French, to eight. The stanza above proceeds line-by-line, but enjambement becomes more common as the spiritual struggle intensifies: the 'G' stanza begins 'Glorious mayde and mooder, which that nevere / Were bitter...'. The final quatrain of the final stanza returns us to our starting point, the petitioning of 'merciable' Mary:

Now, ladi bryghte, sith thou canst and wilt	*since*
Ben to the seed of Adam merciable,	*be merciful*
Bring us to that palais that is bilt	*palace that is built*
To penitentes that ben to merci able. Amen	*for penitents receptive*

(181–4)

The poem ends with *rime riche*, an effect that pairs identical sounds with differing grammatical functions ('merciable' and 'merci able'); Mary's 'might' is thus realized as both adjectival (an attribute) and adverbial (a way of acting). An *ABC* shows sophisticated acquaintance with legal terminology as the speaker pleads his case, as if in a law court, and oscillates more freely than its source between first person singular ('this is all about me') and first person plural ('this is about all of us'). And yet this poem, which appears as the first of Chaucer's 'Short Poems' in the standard *Riverside Chaucer* edition, was long thought to be one of his earliest and most 'unambitious' compositions. How could this be?

The man who judged it 'unambitious' and, in the absence of any real evidence, 'quite an early work' was the Reverend William Walter Skeat (1835–1912), the most influential editor and etymologizer of Middle English in the nineteenth century and, perhaps, ever. Skeat, the first Cambridge professor to ride a bicycle and the father of six children, was embarrassed by the *ABC* as a petitionary prayer to the Blessed Virgin Mary since such devotion, according to Victorian Anglican thinking, betokens spiritual infancy, a preoccupation of immature years. Chaucer, however, persisted with Marian prayer throughout his career: the *Man of Law's Tale*, told by a top-ranking lawyer, pivots on an intense Marian petition (2.841–61), and even *T&C*, his tale of pagan Troy, ends with Mary ('mayde and mooder') in its final line (5.1869). Mary also appears in the prayer or 'retraction' with which Chaucer 'taketh . . . his leve' at the end of *CT*. In the last months of his life, Chaucer lived at Westminster among Benedictine monks; he chose to be buried among them, rather than in the more public part of the Abbey.

It is no simple matter to access Chaucer's religion. We are separated from Chaucer not just by the Reformation, but by the Counter-Reformation too: that process through which the Catholic church, no longer relaxedly confident in its universalist claims, lost its sense of humour. Dante, Boccaccio, and Petrarch seemed suddenly impious, or unfunny; nuns in sixteenth-century Europe were locked behind high walls. Attempts to enclose nuns more strictly in fourteenth-century England, following a papal bull, failed miserably; the Chaucerian company travelling to

Canterbury includes two tale-telling sisters (plus one just along for the ride). The range of Christian belief expressed by Chaucer's pilgrims is remarkably broad, ranging from the orthodox perfectionism embraced by professional religious, such as the nuns, to its explicit rejection ('that am nat I', 3.118) by the Wife of Bath, and others. The variety of belief explored in Chaucer's writing is, by any standard, extraordinary. Such exploratory freedom went missing in sixteenth-century England. Consider one question that recurs in Chaucer, and in the poetry of his fourteenth-century contemporaries: what happens to good people, who happen not to be any kind of Christian, when they die? Sixteenth-century England, so sharply divided between Protestant and Catholic belief, and between varieties of belief within Protestantism, showed little inclination to head down this exploratory road.

Paganism

One of Chaucer's most celebrated scenes sees a newly deceased pagan prince, Troilus, look down upon the world from a great height. What, readers wonder, will become of this Trojan knight, loyal in love to the end? Chaucer supplies no answer, but he certainly registers the question:

> And forth he wente, shortly for to telle, *long story short*
> Ther as Mercurye sorted hym to dwelle. *assigned*
> (5.1826–7)

Chaucer's next lines here are presented in this way by modern editions, but not by medieval manuscripts:

> Swich fyn hath, lo, this Troilus for love!   *such an ending*
> Swich fyn hath al his grete worthynesse!   *great*
>
> (5.1828–9)

Medieval scribes did not use exclamation marks, and so it is important to reread these lines without them. The effect of beginning five successive lines with anaphora (repetition of the same word) and ending each with exclaiming (!!!!!) is to suggest histrionics in a speaker abandoning, finally, his hero. Without exclamation marks the mood is gentler, sadder, and more meditative, leaving open the question: what *will* happen to this lover of great worthiness beyond the grave? Similar thoughts arise as we hear from another worthy pagan, Arcite, as he lies dying in the *Knight's Tale*:

> 'What is this world? What asketh men to have?
> Now with his love, now in his colde grave   *at one moment*
> Allone, withouten any compaignye'.
>
> (1.2777–9)

Arcite is a young knight from ancient Thebes, a city associated by Chaucer and his classical sources with cycles of historical disaster. Earlier in the poem, Arcite had tried to puzzle out what 'purveiaunce of God' (1.252), divine foresight, has in store for him. He apprehends that a human being *does* have a spiritual home somewhere, but, like a drunk who has mislaid his house key, he cannot remember quite where:

> 'A dronke man woot wel he hath an hous,   *knows well that*
> But he noot which the righte wey is thider,   *does not know   there*
> And to a dronke man the wey is slider'.   *way   slippery*
>
> (1.1262–4)

Arcite's cousin and rival in love, Palemon, accuses the 'cruel goddes' of sticking rigidly to their plans, and of indifference to human suffering: we humans cower, he says, like sheep in the sheepfold (1.1308). This may have resonated with Chaucer's readers, mindful that the divine plan for England in 1348 was, apparently, to kill one in three. But while many might *think* such thoughts, few would dare voice them: unless, of course, they were reading Chaucer aloud—and medieval texts were almost always read aloud. Chaucer's Thebans and Trojans are recognizably fourteenth-century Londoners, in light disguise; London, we have noted, referred to itself as 'New Troy'. In setting so many of his tales among pagans, distant from medieval London in time, geography, or both, Chaucer enters realms of questioning where his readers dared not travel in everyday life.

Seint Erkenwald, an alliterative poem written by one of Chaucer's most talented contemporaries, is similarly audacious. In seventh-century London, East Saxons, or early Londoners, are dismantling a pagan temple with a view to building the first St Paul's Cathedral. On finding a richly decorated tomb, they jimmy open the lid and discover the perfectly preserved body of a king. Erkenwald, the local bishop, dialogues with this corpse and then weeps with compassion for its lost pagan soul. A single tear 'trillyd adoun' (322), falling onto the dead man's face; this has the force of baptism, and the good pagan is saved. This is cleverly worked, since Erkenwald both does and does not save this lost soul: he was not to know that his tear, wept from human compassion, would be graced with sacramental

91

power. Dante is similarly ingenious in *Paradiso* 20 in discovering Ripheus, a Trojan, in the heaven of justice (lines 67–72). How does Dante get away with this? By observing that, according to Vergil's *Aeneid*, Ripheus was 'iustissimus unus', most just among the Trojans (2.427). A man judged 'iustissimus' by Vergil properly belongs, Dante deduces, in the heaven of justice. He keeps company there with the Roman emperor Trajan, a non-Judaic pagan who pops up more widely in medieval literature, including *Piers Plowman*, the great visionary poem written in the same alliterative tradition as *Seint Erkenwald*.

In his *Commedia*, Dante is doubly audacious in ways clearly appreciated by Chaucer's *T&C*. Firstly, Dante proposes that the love that a man feels for a woman (not his wife) might lead towards salvation; and secondly, that careful reading of texts written by pagans, such as Vergil, might align with this upward movement. In the Earthly Paradise, a strangely mixed, classical-Christian terrain, Dante passes from the care of the pagan Vergil to Beatrice, his earthly but now heavenly beloved (*Purgatorio* cantos 28–33). In the middle book of *T&C*, Chaucer similarly explores this mysterious boundary between pagan virtue and Christian salvation. On finally achieving the love of Criseyde, Troilus sends up a prayer, a vote of thanks, to 'Benigne Love, thow holy bond of thynges' (3.1261). This whole stanza, remarkably, models itself on *Paradiso* 33.14–18, St Bernard's address to the Virgin Mary; it is here and now, in this very last canto, that Dante, reunited with Beatrice, finally glimpses how the love he feels for and with her might align with 'the love that moves the sun and the other stars' (33.145). Troilus, newly

united with Criseyde, and in a part of Chaucer's poem thick
with classical and Dantean allusions, hopes for something
similar in continuing his paean of praise to 'Benigne Love':

'And for thow me, that koude leest disserve	*because least deserving*
Of hem that noumbred ben unto thi grace,	*those preselected your*
Hast holpen, ther I likly was to sterve,	*helped likely to die*
And me bistowed in so heigh a place	*high*
That thilke boundes may no blisse pace,	*that boundary exceed*
I kan namore; but laude and reverence	*am capable of praise*
Be to thy bounte and thyn excellence!'	

(3.1268–74)

The middle line of this stanza is in fact the middle line of the
entire poem, the 4120st of the 8239. At this plateau, this
'high place', it seems that Troilus has been led by his whole-
hearted pursuit of love to something like salvation: by
'grace' he is 'numbered' among the elect. And he is content
to rest at this 'boundary', and simply to give praise to
'Benign Love'. But all is downhill from here. This pagan
may, like Dante's Vergil, have been granted a glimpse of
Christian truth, but he is not, finally, guaranteed to dwell
in it; the narrator will turn sharply away from him at the
end, disavowing 'payens corsed olde rites' (5.1849). And yet
what the poem has dared to dream or surmise, close to its
midpoint, lingers in the mind.

Six of Chaucer's Canterbury tales are set in pagan times,
or pagan locales, while three more share Christian and
non-Christian terms of reference. Since low-life tellers
favour present-day tales, with the Manciple an interesting

exception, this represents a high percentage of Chaucer's serious imaginative output. Barriers between Christian and pagan terms of reference are generally porous, and this is not because Chaucer, as a medieval poet, blunders into anachronism (see p. 67). Protagonists such as Dorigen in the *Franklin's Tale*, which sees a young squire pray to both sun and moon, seem just like us, in fancy dress, period or regional. And yet Chaucer, like some of his thinking contemporaries, clearly worried that many good people, distant in time or space, may not be numbered among 'hem at the day of doom that shulle be saved' (10.1092). These are the last words, barring scribal formulae, of his *Canterbury Tales*.

Judaism

As the oldest, most fundamental of the three major monotheisms, the status of Judaism is unique, and uniquely vexed: for it is both *internal to* Christianity and Islam, and yet (to a greater or lesser extent) disavowed by them. Judaism cannot be dispensed with, and neither—at least for St Augustine (354–430 CE)—could Jews, for they serve to remind Christians, Augustine argues, whence Christianity came. Jewish people were thus assigned a function within the economy of Christian salvation, and their mass conversion would signal the onset of 'end times', the apocalypse. Since they were generally denied the right to participate in market economies regulated by Christians, Jews specialized in one aspect of the market that was, for Christians, off-limits: the lending of money. The commodity being paid for in moneylending, medieval theologians reasoned, was time, and time could not be bought or sold, since time is the gift of God. The lending of money, or the selling of time, was defined as usury, a mortal sin. Such arguments slackened with the passage of time, and the rise of capitalism, and in 1605, the year of the first recorded performance of Shakespeare's *Merchant of Venice*, Pope Paul V founded *Il Banco di Santo Spirito*; this 'bank of the Holy Spirit' lasted until 1992, when it merged with the *Banca di Roma*. This change of attitude towards moneylending, one of Catholicism's most spectacular U-turns, was accompanied by changing attitudes towards Jews. It is no accident that the boom years of the medieval economy, roughly 1100–1300, coincided with a sharpening of anti-Semitic arguments. Peter the Venerable (*c.*1092–1156) reasoned that any reasonable person who reads Scripture *must* see the truth of Christian revelation. Anyone *not* seeing it must therefore be wilfully blind, or lacking in reason; and to lack reason is to be little better than a beast. It is to illustrate the first of these arguments that *Synagoga*, as depicted by gentiles in this period, often wears a blindfold. The syllogisms or logical linkages that structure Peter the Venerable's argument owe much to Aristotle. Aristotle's increasing presence in the West itself owed much to Jewish translators, most especially in Toledo, who worked between Madrasah teachers (much of Aristotle had been translated from Greek to Arabic) and Latin-literate Cluniac monks. Here, as so often, Jews performed a mediatory role, vital to Christian society, that exposed them to persecution from Christian society: as with moneylending, so with the transmission of knowledge.

The large Jewish community that formed in London after 1066, very likely translated from Rouen, helped to supply the financial credit that bedded down the Norman Conquest. This community gradually expanded outward from London, generating urban settlements in places such as Hertford, Bedford, Cambridge, and Colchester. Eventually, there were twenty-four provincial Jewries in England, including Oxford, Hereford, Worcester, and Gloucester, as well as more isolated, and hence vulnerable, communities at places such as Lincoln, Norwich, and York. Jewish communities favoured urban settings, but with extensive local networking: Cambridgeshire villagers from Babraham, Caxton, Grantchester, Histon, and Madingley, for example, would travel to Cambridge if they needed a loan. The texts and objects from which we might reconstruct the everyday lives of Jewish people in England have generally gone missing, although some do come to light during the building of sites such as the Cambridge Corn Exchange. What mostly remains of early Jewish history in England is a succession of dates indicating persecution, pogrom, and finally, expulsion. In 1144, the discovery of a 12-year-old boy's body outside Norwich led to accusations against the Jewish community, formation of a Christian cult, and then *The Life and Passion of William of Norwich*, composed by a local monk. In 1190, with Richard I ('the Lionheart') en route to Jerusalem, riots against local 'infidels' spread from London to Norwich and Lincoln before precipitating the death of York's entire Jewish population. In 1265, the disappearance of another Christian boy led to the hanging of Henry III's Jewish steward, Copin of Lincoln, and the execution of eighteen more Lincoln Jews in London. The cult of 'Hugh of Lincoln' was vigorously promoted, and a plaque attesting to his supposed martyrdom (Jews in fact had nothing to do with his death) could be found in the Cathedral until 1959. Philippa Chaucer was admitted to the Fraternity of Lincoln Cathedral on 19 February 1386, along with John of Gaunt and his son, the future Henry IV.

Chaucer's Prioress concludes her tale by declaring that the slaying of 'yonge Hugh of Lyncoln' by 'cursed Jewes' happened 'but a litel while ago' (7.684–6). In looking back to 1265, surely more than 'a little while ago', the Prioress over-leaps a crucial date: 1290, the year in which Jews had been expelled from England. That is to say, there had been no Jewish community in England for a century before the Canterbury *compaignye* set out (and Jews would not return until 1655). So what the Prioress gives us in her tale, set vaguely 'in Asye, in a greet citee' (7.488), is an anti-Semitism uncontaminated by actual contact with Jewish people. Her performance is not 'about' Jews at all, but is rather what Miri Rubin calls 'a gentile tale', issuing from the anxieties of non-Jews. To try and understand what these anxieties might be, in the case of the Prioress, is not to try and get her (or Chaucer) off the hook: there can be no 'saving' a society from something integral to its cultural fabric. But the ferocity of the Prioress's schizophrenic animal loving/Jew hating does beg some explanation. *GP* pictures her feeding her lapdogs tidbits and weeping at dead or bleeding mice (1.142–50), whereas her tale imagines Jews being dragged by wild horses and then hanged—not just those who commit-ted the crime, but anyone who knew about it ('that of this mordre wiste', 7.630). What anxieties might feed such tenderness and ferocity? Perhaps the Prioress is stirred by the vulnerability of her child protagonist; the term *litel* appears fourteen times in her short tale, nine times attached to him. Curiously, however, the Prioress represents herself (to the Virgin Mary) as less or smaller than the 'litel clergeoun',

> ...as a child of twelf month oold, or lesse,   *twelve months old*
> That kan unnethes any word expresse,   *hardly knows how to*
> Right so fare I...
>
> (7.484–6)

A clue to what *really* feels under threat to the Prioress is given by the Latin rubric immediately preceding her tale, and her opening half-line (which translates it): '*Domine dominus noster*'; 'O Lord, oure Lord'. This is from Psalm 8, which opened matins in the Little Office of the Virgin, and also supplied the introit for the Mass of the Holy Innocents. Matins is the day's first service for the Prioress and her nuns, who gather to sing in their convent eight times every day. Such singing is *beautiful*: small wonder that the 'litel clergeoun', apprentice singer, has his heart stolen by *Alma Redemptoris Mater*. So any group resistant to the charm and persuasive force of such singing must be very wicked indeed: Jews, for example. Gregorian chant, where the assembled *compaignye* (those eating of the same bread) sing one line in unison, suggests a one-faith world of *harmony within*; trouble lies outside, beyond the boundaries of the choir, Church, and (after 1290) nation. Guillaume de Machaut, however, set out with his polyvocal *Messe de Notre Dame* to explore strange harmonies and seeming discords within the body of sacred music, the Catholic mass. With French *ars nova*, as the new style was termed, Western Europe engages with its own internal discords. Jewish people hearing such music in the fourteenth century, were such a thing possible, might find polyvocal Machaut more reassuring than monophonic Gregorian chant.

Christianity

Ironically, the *Prioress's Tale*, which has Satan directly addressing 'Hebrayk peple' (7.560), twice makes use of typology, the device which sees an 'Old Testament' figure fulfilled in the New (hence proving the indispensability of the Jewish Bible): the burning but unconsumed bush that appears to Moses in Exodus 3.2 prefigures Mary's perpetual virginity (7.468), and the mother lamenting her still-singing son becomes 'this newe Rachel' (7.627; Jeremiah 31.15). Such superimposition of time schemes, a routine yet remarkable feature of medieval imagining, persists in the tale told by the Prioress's convent companion, the nameless Second Nun. This is set in the time of 'goode Urban the old', 'Seint Urban', 'hooly olde Urban' (8.177, 179, 185). The pope repeatedly referenced here, the first of that name (Urban I, 222–30 CE), plies his heroic trade of Christian leadership at Rome in the face of imperial persecution; he hides among catacombs (8.186). The Second Nun writes, however, during the pontificate of Pope Urban VII (1378–89), at a time when Western Christendom had split between rival popes. England sided with the Roman papacy (but Scotland with the popes of Avignon), so Chaucer scores some diplomatic points by honouring long-pedigreed Urbanism. Yet even in doing so, he reminds us of schism, and of the great gulf between heroic early Roman Catholicism and its current tawdry present.

Female listeners might further notice the great gap between the active life of the tale's protagonist, Cecelie, leading an apostolate of the streets, and their own attenuated religious lives. The Second Nun is her own translator (such is her 'feithful bisynesse', 8.24), but male translators of her chief source text, the *Legenda aurea* or *Golden Legend* by Jacobus de Voragine, worried that modern women might get ideas above their station if inspired by the likes of St Cecelia; their advice was *don't try this at home*. Women who contemplate Mary Magdalene preaching, as described by the *Legenda aurea*, clearly see new possibilities (Figure 11).

One of *CT*'s most exhilarating verbal exchanges pits Cecelie, who sees the truth clearly, against Almachius, the pagan Roman prefect, who does not. She totally pricks his balloon:

Almachius seyde, 'Ne takestow noon heede	*aren't you impressed by*
Of my power?' and she answerde hym this:	
'Youre might', quod she, 'ful litel is to dreed,	*is nothing much to worry about*
For every mortal mannes power nys	*every mortal man's power is*
But lyk a bladdre ful of wynd, ywys.	*but a bladder full of wind*
For with a nedles poynt, whan it is blowe,	*a needleprick, when inflated*
May al the boost of it be leyd ful lowe'.	*boast be deflated*

(8.435–41)

Cecelie had earlier claimed, on her wedding night, to have a jealous angel watching over her; any husbandly encroachment (Margery Kempe, would-be East Anglian mystic, loved

Figure 11 Mary Magdalene Preaching, oil on panel, Netherlands, c.1500–20, Philadelphia Museum of Art, John G. Johnson Collection, 1917. Scene from the *Legenda aurea*, set outside Marseilles, with the cross-branch between the trees discreetly suggesting a pulpit. Recognized as *apostle to the apostles* in the Middle Ages, since the resurrected Christ first appeared to her, Mary Magdalene was granted an official Catholic feast day in 2016.

this story) will be punished by death (8.152–61). Valerian, Cecelie's newly wedded spouse, is understandably keen to have hard evidence: 'Lat me that aungel se' (8.164). In the tale-world of the Second Nun, he gets it: an old man dressed in white stands before him holding a book with gold lettering (8.200–3). In such a world, where evidence stares you in the face, it is easy to be clear-sighted: 'Whoso that troweth nat this', says Valerian's brother, Tiburce, 'a beest he is' (6.288). But in saying that 'he who does not believe this is an animal', Tiburce loops us back into the anti-Semitism of Peter the Venerable (see p. 95), the image of wilfully blind *Synagoga*, and the overt anti-Semitism of the Second Nun's Prioress. What might exhilarate and reassure some readers is for others a sign of danger.

The final stanza of the *Second Nun's Tale* sees 'Seint Urban' turning the house where 'Seint Cecelie' has died into a church, still to be seen in Rome 'into this day' (8.552). We thus return from the first Urban to the current one; from the age of charismatic individuals to the routinization of charisma, to institutionalization and bureaucracy. Some religious thinkers of Chaucer's time yearned to release the Church from such sclerotic clutter, to return to its simpler, pristine state. Chaucer's most religiously idealized pilgrims live simply and well: the Parson tends his flock close to home, and his Plowman brother pays his tithes and spreads dung for the common good (1.530). When the Parson's orthodox zeal prompts him to object to excessive swearing, the Host is unimpressed: '"O Jankin, be ye there? / I smelle a Lollere in the wynd", quod he' (2.1172–3). This passage, along with the rest of the epilogue following *The*

Man of Law's Tale, was later cut from the most authoritative manuscripts. Had such reference to Lollardy, the incipient church reform movement, become too hot to handle? Perhaps, but the cutting of this muddled epilogue had more to do with the evolving tale-telling order of *CT*. The Host's association of Lollardy with mere prissy piety, as he sees it, is in any case not very accurate, and his jocular sloppiness a sign of the times. Some years later, when Margery Kempe hit the road, it was crucial to know who or what 'a Lollere' was—but by then, Chaucer was safely dead and buried.

Before dying, Cecelie lives between life and death for three days. Her neck has been struck three times by her executioner's blade, but since a fourth blow is forbidden 'by ordinaunce' (8.529) she is left to bleed slowly to death. In living thus liminally (see the final section of this chapter) she shares the condition of an anchoress—who is dead to the world, walled into her cell, yet able to speak back *to* the world, and 'to teche' (8.538). In 1373, while Chaucer was making momentous literary discoveries in Italy, a 30-year-old woman in East Anglia was experiencing near-death visions; she then spent decades pondering their meaning. Julian of Norwich and Chaucer likely never met (but who knows?), and they are rarely considered together as English writers. Yet they do work away at certain common questions, approached very differently, such as *what love is* and *how love works*. Both mythologize superbly, although Julian is more audacious: while Chaucer tells why women have an answer in any crisis (p. 38), Julian rewrites the fall of man as a parable of overeagerness to please God. Julian thinks more brilliantly, but this is unfair: nobody *thinks* more brilliantly and originally in English than Julian of Norwich.

Islam

The English monk-historian William of Malmesbury (*c*.1090–*c*.1142, Anglo-Norman by parentage, writing in Latin) tells in his *Gesta Regum Anglorum* of a young monk, prompted by boredom or ambition, running off to Spain to learn astrology and other arts from the Saracens. Having made a devil's pact to obtain and keep a secret Saracen book full of arcane knowledge, he enjoys a brilliant career as necromancer and, finally, pope (Sylvester II, 999–1003) before death and damnation. Chaucer's Franklin knows a good deal about astrology, but also knows that such knowledge is suspect. Having assured us that 'I ne kan no termes of astologye' (5.1266), he shows virtuosic knowledge of just such 'termes' before disavowing them again as

. . . swich illusiouns and swich meschaunces	*such*
As hethen folk useden in thilke dayes.	*heathen practised*
	those

(5.1292–3)

Among the tools used by the Franklin's young astrologer are 'tables Tolletanes' (5.1273), astronomical tables adjusted to the longitude of Toledo, the city in Castile which had seen intensive collaboration between Muslim, Christian, and Arab scholars bent on migrating Greek learning (often in Arabic translation) westwards. The 'tables Tolletanes' succeeded earlier tables compiled by Al-Zargali of Cordova (rendered by Chaucer as 'Arsechieles' in his *Astrolabe*, 2.45.2) and were themselves later adapted for use in other cities—including London. Use of such 'tables', as Chaucer teaches his young 'sone' Lewis, can help fix and plot planetary positions into the future. Calculations later on in *A Treatise on the Astrolabe* involve 'the yer of oure Lord 1400' (2.45.38–9). This, it turns out, would be the year of Chaucer's death. Which might remind us of the comment by John, the old Oxford carpenter of the *Miller's Tale*, as another stargazing astronomer tumbles into a clay pit: 'he saugh nat that' (*he didn't see that coming*, 1.3461).

Elsewhere in Oxford we may still find a copy of Al-Zargali or 'Arsechieles' once owned by William Rede, Bishop of Chichester (d.1385), safely locked away in Merton College Library (MS 259). Merton was home to the so-called 'Oxford Calculators' of the fourteenth century, a group dedicated to mathematics and mechanics, and to developing the work on trigonometry of Al-Battani (*c*.858–929 CE), another Arab astronomer. Arabic-derived scientific procedure pervades another of the *CT* treading dangerous ground, namely the *Canon's Yeoman's Tale*. The Canon's teaching on 'the four spirites and the bodies seven' (8.820), itself deriving from Al-Razi (*c*.826–925 CE), is fundamentally important for an alchemist dealing with volatile substances ('spirites') and metals ('bodies'). Al-Razi, or Abu Bakr Muhammad ibn Zakariyya, was known to the Latin West as Rhazes, one of many names which helped familiarize, almost naturalize, Arab names in the West: thus Ṣalāḥ ad-Dīn Yūsuf ibn Ayyūb became Saladin, the greatest of warriors, the Persian polymath Abū 'Alī al-Ḥusayn ibn 'Abd Allāh ibn Al-Hasan ibn Ali ibn Sīnā became Avicenna, and ʾAbū l-Walīd Muḥammad Ibn ʾAḥmad Ibn Rušd, the great commentator on Aristotle, became Averroes. All three of these appear among the virtuous pagans of Dante's Limbo (*Inferno* 4), and Averroes features remarkably again in 'The Triumph of Thomas Aquinas', painted at Florence just a few years before Chaucer's arrival (Figure 12). His awkward yet central accommodation in this fresco argues, tacitly, 'can't fit me in, can't leave me out'.

Dante's alchemists appear very deep in his scheme of hell. Their art was regarded as exceptionally dangerous for reasons both social (success would destroy a gold-based economy) and theological: men should not peer too deeply, to again cite John the Oxford carpenter, into 'Goddes pryvetee', *God's private parts*, 1.3454). And yet the allure of 'the elvysshe craft' (8.751), with its multiplying of strange and exotic vocabularies, was clearly compelling—at least to Chaucer. In trying to evoke the look on the pilgrim Chaucer's face, his 'contenaunce', the Host comes up with 'elvyssh' (7.703), a unique collocation suggesting perhaps that striving for *poesye*, at least in English, is like trying to turn base metal into gold. And perhaps, after all, it can be done: the very end of the *Canon's Yeoman's Tale* takes a surprisingly hopeful turn, conceding that, yes, there *is* a secret to be learned. It's just that Christ 'wol nat that it discovered be' (8.1468), liking to divulge his secret as and when he sees fit. This last revelation (of non- or selective revelation) is attributed to a book called 'Senior' (8.1450), yet another Westernized and Christianized version of a

Figure 12 Andrea di Bonaiuto (*c.*1365), Averroes sitting at the feet of St Thomas Aquinas, Spanish Chapel, Santa Maria Novella, Florence.

Muslim name, in this case the Cordoban Muhammed ibn Umail al-Tamîmî (*c.*900–60 CE).

In *Sir Thopas*, the tale that Chaucer assigns to himself, the eponymous hero takes a bumpy ride into fairyland on clunking, tail-rhyme metre:

Til that ther cam a greet geaunt,	*great giant*
His name was sire Olifaunt,	*Sir Elephant*
A perilous man of dede.	*in his deeds*
He seyde, 'Child, by Termagaunt,	
But if thou prike out of myn haunt,	*unless you ride out of my territory*
Anon I sle thy steede	*I'll brain your horse*
With mace'.	*with a mace*

(7.807)

Termagant, a name borne by seven Royal Navy fighting ships between 1780 and 1965, has come to mean 'a feisty woman'. Hamlet recalls her ranting style in mystery plays when speaking of an actor's 'ore-doing (*overdoing*) Termagant; it out Herods Herod' (3.2.13–14). Originally, however, Termagant was a female deity imagined by medieval Christians to form part, along with Roman Apollo and the prophet Muhammed, of an Islamic Trinity. This bizarre troika famously shows up in the *Song of Roland*—where Saracens mix with giants, and much depends upon the blowing of an 'olifant'. Such 'Saracen' Trinities also appear in the tail-rhyme romances parodied by *Sir Thopas*, but not in Chaucer's serious fiction; 'Mahoun' is referred to singly as 'our prophete' (2.224), 'Goddes message' (*messenger*, 2.333), and 'oure creaunce' (*our faith*, 2.340). One curious exception, how-ever, comes towards the very end of *T&C*:

| Lo here, the fyn and guerdoun for travaille | *ending and reward for labour* |
| Of Jove, Appollo, of Mars, of swich rascaille. | *of such rascality* |

(5.1852–3; repunctuated)

The notion that any non-Christian religion should config-ure a Trinity clearly projects one of Christianity's stranger doctrines, Trinitarianism, onto other faiths; Christian apolo-gists found it perennially hard to explain their God-who-is-not-one to Jews and Muslims. It is curious that Chaucer should evoke such a 'shadow Trinity' here, just ten lines before his orthodox Trinitarian closure, borrowed from Dante. This final stanza of *T&C* begins:

| Thow oon, and two, and thre, eterne on lyve, | *living eternally* |
| That regnest ay in thre, and two, and oon | *forever reigns* |

(5.1863–4)

The term 'rascaille' of 5.1853 is worth returning to, in this context, for its hunting metaphor: *rascaille* are deer too young to kill, so pursuit of them sends hunters down the wrong track. In conceiving of Trinities, so medieval Christians imagined, Muslims grasped some glimmerings of truth; Islam is thus popularly pictured in the Middle Ages as a mis-taken parody of Christianity, rather than as something quite alien, evoking *otherness*. Saracen princesses, in Middle English romances, enjoy wild adventures that English girls could only dream of before, without much trouble, finding the right (mar-riage) path, and becoming Christian. Whereas Judaism is ante-cedent to, internal to, and contemporaneous with Christianity, Islam is a younger sibling. And one that Chaucer generally treats with respect: the Man of Law's Syrian merchants are 'sadde and trewe' (*steadfast and honest*, two of Chaucer's most positive epithets, 2.135), and according to the Squire, the Tartar Cambyuskan keeps his 'lay', his law, his faith (5.18).

The Squire's father, Chaucer's Knight, has beaten the bounds of Dar al-Islam, travelling (like many a Muslim cleric) from Morocco in the west to Alexandria, along the Maghrib, but then also crossing to Granada and Algeciras in Al-Andalus before winding around the Mediterranean to locations in Turkey (1.43–69). His son has stayed closer to home but travels in imagination yet further afield, telling of the 'queynte mirours' of 'Alocen' (Ibn al-Haitham, an expert on optics born in Basra *c*.965 CE; *CT* 5.232–4). The Squire's tale of romance wonders is set 'at Sarray' (5.9), now Tsarev (near Volgograd), then capital of the Golden Horde. The prolific Moroccan traveller Ibn Battuta had passed through this cosmopolitan Muslim-Christian city in the 1330s before heading to Samarkand, Delhi, Calicut, Sumatra, and the east coast of China; regions that Mandeville fakes having seen, in his *Book of Travels and Marvels*, are carefully described. In Chaucer's lifetime, Ibn Khaldun (1332–1406) both travelled and theorized the dynamics between sedentary and nomadic civilizations in ways that look back to Geoffrey of Monmouth and forwards to modern sociology. In 1401, he was lowered down in a basket from the walls of Damascus to negotiate with the besieging Timur the Lame ('Tamerlane'); their discussions took weeks and fill many pages. In 1402, Timur defeated the Ottoman Sultan Bayezid I at Ankara. Readers of Mandeville's *Travels and Marvels* hoped that salvation might come, *in extremis*, from a Christian emperor of the East called

Prester John, but in 1402 it was a Mongol khan who bought Constantinople fifty years of respite. Chaucer was dead by then, but a steady flow of visitors from the East, such as his Knight, would earlier have fed his appreciation of Islamic civilizations, sophisticated and various. Sufism and science, not the Wahhabist fundamentalism of later centuries, are hallmark qualities of fourteenth-century European Islam.

Our Planet, Our Home

On emerging from Hell's darkness onto the shores of Purgatory, Dante delights in seeing a luminously radiant planet in the sky, a 'bel pianeto' (1.19). This is Venus, the 'beautiful planet', thought literally to *in-fluence* (by 'flowing in') human susceptibility to love and (for Dante) rhetoric, and hence poetry. Dante is not 'at home' on planet Earth, but is rather ascending to the heavens, true home of every human soul. Each soul, the poet Statius explains later in *Purgatorio*, is breathed into a human embryo by God, 'the first mover', only when said embryo has developed through vegetable (it is said first to resemble a sea-fungus, 'spungo marino', 25.56), and then animal stages. Dante, a political exile, naturally longs to return to his place of birth, Florence, but his soul's greater longing is for heaven, his true home. Similar longing is expressed by the Marian antiphon *Salve Regina*, a companion piece to the *Alma Redemptoris Mater* sung by the Prioress's 'clergeon'. Having hailed ('Salve') Mary as queen ('regina') of heaven, the singer maps collective alienation:

111

> Ad te clamamus exsules filii Hevæ,
> Ad te suspiramus, gementes et flentes
> in hac lacrimarum valle.

> To you we cry, poor banished sons of Eve,
> To you we sigh, mourning and weeping
> In this valley of tears.

(3–5)

These lines are translated feelingly by Chaucer's Second Nun as she prepares for poetic labour as an 'unworthy sone of Eve':

Now help, thow meeke and blisful faire mayde,
Me, flemed wrecche, in this desert of galle.   *exiled wretch*
                                                 bitterness

(8.57–8, 62)

This seems entirely at odds with contemporary sensibility. Our poor planet is not the centre of the universe, but rather a small and vulnerable 'third rock from the sun' that is overheating, depleting, and heading for possible (human) extinction. Modern humans have evolved for more than a million years with and through the planet; they may feel alienated as medievals do, but this is not (for most) because their souls originated elsewhere. Medievals and moderns do, however, share intensive concern with nature, or Nature. For Chaucer, Nature, encountered as 'a noble emperesse' in the garden of his *Parliament of Fowls*, is 'the vicaire of the almyghty Lord' (309, 379), and for Dante, this makes the human artist, imitating nature, 'the grandchild of God' (*Inferno* 11.105). And yet the first humans, according to

Genesis, were dropped into the garden of a completed Nature; natural order precedes human attempts at social organization. There are hints in Chaucer, as in other medieval texts, of worlds more ancient than human worlds, and of native traditions of belief, ancient and mysterious, overlaid or co-opted by Christianity. The Wife of Bath briefly evokes a time of dancing elf-queens (3.860), and the magical lady-protagonist of her *Tale* is found sitting 'on the grene' (3.998; 3.1047). Chaucer's Reeve lives on a heath 'shadowed by green trees' (1.607), and his intimate knowledge of the landscape he manages is indispensable. The most celebrated celebration of greenness in Chaucer's England is that of *Sir Gawain and the Green Knight*, a poem in which a sprig of holly, 'more green than ever when woods are bare' (207), proves more potent than Gawain's pentangle, the fanciest of Christian devices. Chaucer allows us a brief glimpse of a secret green world just as it is disappearing, as a massive logging operation bares the landscape to serve human needs. This description, in the *Knight's Tale*, is negatively framed, part of a long list of things we will *not* be told about:

Ne hou the goddes ronnen up and doun,	*how run*
Disherited of hire habitacioun,	*disinherited from*
In which they woneden in reste and pees,	*lived peace*
Nymphes, fawnes and amadrides.	*Hamadryads [wood nymphs]*

(1.2925–8)

The lines immediately following are more remarkable still. During a medieval harvest, animals would cluster together in diminishing space, as the scythes worked towards

113

them, before making a bolt for it. Something similar is pictured here:

Ne hou the beestes and the briddes alle	*how beasts birds*
Fledden for fere, whan the wode was falle;	*fear wood*
Ne how the ground agast was of the light,	*was frightened by*
That was nat wont to seen the sonne bright.	*not accustomed*

(1.2929–32)

This remarkable switching of viewing perspective finds us looking *with* the earth, rather than at it, as the tree canopy is removed and sunlight strikes for the first time. Chaucer here anticipates a foundational act of modern eco-criticism: to imagine that the planet that we inhabit, and are laying to waste, might itself have a point of view.

Thresholds, Portals to Beyond

The concluding part of the *Second Nun's Tale*, we have noted, sees Cecelie poised between life and death for three days of bleeding and teaching. Such was the space occupied by an anchoress, such as Julian of Norwich, from the day she was bricked into her cell. She had three windows: one to the altar, another for her servants, and another to the world. Anyone, such as Margery Kempe of Lynn, could come to visit; the anchoress was always home, occupying her liminal or borderline space as the poorest yet most potent of creatures. Her words, connecting the living and the dead, have peculiar charge. *Limen* in Latin means literally 'a threshold', and its strangeness as a space is reaffirmed for us when someone rings the doorbell: 'come in', we might say, or perhaps not—in which case, hopefully, they will leave. Things must be decided either way; conversation *at the threshold* feels awkward, time-compressed.

Through liminal markers, Chaucer signals to his reader (but usually not to his protagonist) the onset of supernatural encounters. When the knight-rapist of the *Wife of Bath's Tale* sees a group of women 'by a forest side' (3.990), between open and wooded ground, something magical is afoot; when the Summoner of the *Friar's Tale* sees a yeoman on horseback 'under a forest side' (3.1380), we know (but the Summoner does not) that we are entering a metaphysical terrain between life and death, damnation and salvation. A similar point is reached in the *Pardoner's Tale* as three men reach a wooden structure (Figure 13) connecting one open field with another:

Whan they han goon nat fully half a mile,	*had gone not*
Right as they wolde han treden over a stile,	*just as they were about to climb*
An old man and a povre with hem mette.	*poor old man met with them*

(6.711–13)

These protagonists never recognize this liminal marker as signalling entry into a metaphysical world. The old man functions as its *genius loci*, or porter, doomed to dwell at the *limen* of life and death, earth and heaven: 'Leeve moder (*mother*), leet me in' (6.731), he cries, banging on the ground with his staff—but to no avail. The teller of this tale, the Pardoner, is himself at home neither in London nor in Westminster, but in a space between, St Mary Roncevall,

Figure 13 A wooden stile between two distinct spaces, such as this one near Hadrian's Wall, is a powerful liminal site.

an alien priory. Masculine and feminine signs overlap in his body.

The term *threshold* appears three times in *CT*. The *Miller's Tale* sees old John, having found his lodger Nicholas gawping at the air, speak protective prayers and charms 'on the thresshfold of the dore withoute' (1.3482), like a talking *mezuzah*. In the *Clerk's Tale*, Griselde proposes to go stand 'in our doore', and it is from this very place that Walter calls her forth:

And as she wolde over hir threshhold gon,	*was about to cross their/her*
The markis cam and gan hire for to calle,	*marquis her*
And she set doun hir water-pot anon	*down her*
Biside the threshhold, in an oxes stalle	

(4.288–91)

Chaucer rarely repeats himself, so the doubling here of *threshold* is striking, and arresting; something supernatural, between worlds, is playing out. The 'oxes stalle' makes us think of Mary anticipating Jesus. Pregnancy is the ultimate liminal state, and every medieval woman knew herself, when pregnant, to be poised between life and death—like an anchoress. Protestant England would abolish anchorholds, but continue respecting the authorizing power of pregnancy. Many women wrote letters from this liminal space; Elizabeth Joceline's *Legacy to Her Unborn Child* became, once she had died in 1622, a bestseller. Dorigen, in the *Franklin's Tale*, might well fall pregnant if she sleeps with a man who is not her husband. Positioning herself liminally, at the top of a cliff, she contemplates life and death, disgrace or suicide:

Another tyme there wolde she sitte and thinke	
And caste hir eyen dounward fro the brinke.	*her eyes downward*

(5.857–8)

Figure 14 At the sea's edge in *Hamlet*, dir. Laurence Olivier, 1948.

This *limen* between land and sea also *frames* our way into *Hamlet*, forming the place where the ghost (returning from a medieval purgatory) speaks of the hereafter. This scene's most memorable visualization is perhaps Olivier's from 1948, a locus vertiginously reprised just as Hamlet begins 'To be / or not / to be (3.1.58)'; like Dorigen, peering down, he speaks at and of the *limen* between life and death (Figure 14). The most famous filmic realization of this limen, where roiling sea meets dry land, is *The Seventh Seal*, Ingmar Bergman's brilliant account of plague-ravaged, post-Crusade Europe. This is where the knight first sees Death. This limen between earth and sea represents not a one-way passage to

Death, but a place of metaphysical transaction. Custance, of the *Man of Law's Tale*, sails 'into oure occian' and becomes visible to Britons between land and water. She is, by the will of God, stuck in the sand:

And in the sond her ship stiked so fast	*sand*
That thennes wolde it noght of al a tyde;	*would not shift for an entire tide*
The wyl of Crist was that she sholde abyde.	*stay put*

(2.509–11)

Once *un*stuck, Custance lives with Dame Hermengild, the *constabalesse*, and her husband; but it takes a return to this *limen*, as they are out walking 'toward the see' (557), to generate the miracle of Hermengild restoring eyesight to a 'blinde Britoun' (561). This same space later proves the most powerful *limen* of all in unleashing irresistible Marian magic. Sentenced to reboard her boat, Custance launches a mighty and compassionate prayer, declaring Mary's sufferings to be greater than her own, while kneeling 'on the stronde', on the beach (2.841–68). 'Oure Lady' (2.977) will now effectively and invisibly take charge.

The *Nuns' Priest's Tale*, as so often, offers brilliant comic commentary upon such serious matters. Towards the end, Chauntecleer is in a bad way. His father and mother have both been eaten, and he finds himself locked in the jaws of the fox that did the eating. Fox and cock have come to the *edge of a wood*, here certainly a life–death *limen*. Chauntecleer must somehow induce the fox, in this tale all about arts of speech, into an error of *ars dicendi et tacendi*, that is, get him to talk when he should keep his mouth shut. And so he

119

scripts a speech for him, something that he would say, 'if that I were as ye'. In speaking of death, at a place where death seems imminent, Chauntecleer saves himself from death:

'Turneth again, ye proude cherles alle!	*peasants*
A verray pestilence upon yow falle!	*real plague*
Now I am come unto the wodes side,	*edge of a wood*
Maugree youre heed, the cok shal heere abide.	*despite your best efforts*
I wol him ete, in feith, and that anon!'	*will eat him*

(7.3409–13)

Many more liminal sitings remain to be pondered in Chaucer: one thinks of Theseus coming '*almost* unto the toun', where he is arrested by grieving ladies, who, in living with the unburied bones of their husbands, certainly dwell between life and death; or of the alchemical canon, seeking to pry open supernatural secrets 'in the suburbes of a toun' (8.657). Criseyde views Troilus from a window as he enters Troy, fresh and bloody from a skirmish outside ('scarmuch al withoute', 2.611); Troilus latterly haunts the city walls, looking out for a Criseyde who will never return. Analysis might extend to the general design of Chaucer's *Tales*. The tale-telling regime is established not in London, but at the edge of London: at Southwark, just beyond the walls and river. And it dissolves in the final Fragment 'just as we were entering the edge of a village' (10.12). This revisits the *locus* in the *Friar's Tale* when an unsuspecting carter enters town, closely observed by a summoner and a devil in disguise:

> And right at th'entring of the tounes ende
>
> (3.1537)

The carter little suspects that what he *says* here, if aligned with what he *means*, may have serious, anagogical (afterlife) consequences—if not for him, then at least for his horses. The tale's Summoner, later carried away by his devil companion, fails to learn anything here that applies to him. The pilgrims in Chaucer's *compagnye*, even as their collective governance dissolves close to Canterbury, just 'as we were entering the end of a village' (10.12), may not grasp this either. Nor may Chaucer's readers. The individual pilgrim, and reader, may thus end *CT* in a liminal space, between the doomed and the saved, without knowing where they are.

But let us not end with harsh orthodoxy, since many kinds of *limen* are to be found in Chaucer, a sublime poet who explores many forms and objects of belief. New thresholds may arise at any moment of reading: suddenly, the membrane thins between this world and some other.

7

Performance and New Chaucers

Creative responses to Chaucer, across the world, have never been more varied and vibrant. This repairs some shortcomings of earlier centuries, where imitators have generally reworked entrenched ideas of a fatherly, and occasionally misbehaving, Chaucer. Editions of *The Faerie Queen* by Edmund Spenser (1553–99) helped little in proposing a faux-medievalism whose language is stilted and sclerotic (where Chaucer's is endlessly plastic and inventive). Poetic engagement with Dante in English has been similarly underpowered, with only Chaucer, Milton, and Shelley getting seriously to grips with Dante's Italian before more exacting engagements in the last century (Eliot and Pound; Joyce, Beckett, and Heaney; Walcott). Eliot's *Waste Land* opens by proclaiming April, bringer of regeneration in *GP*, to be the cruellest of months. Eliot's counter-Chaucerianism at once assumes familiarity and rebuffs Chaucer, modelling a preference for Dante that persists into *Little Gidding*, where the 'dead master' met in wartime London is Dante's teacher, not Chaucer's. Eliot's championing of Dante as a universal poet, buoyed by a universal Latinity, implicitly ushers Chaucer to the sidelines as the poet (if worthy of the title) of an eccentric, retarded, and hybridized tongue. Ironically, it is these same qualities that now make Chaucer so alluring to poets and performers across our globalized, hybridized world. For if modern English has now replaced Latin as universal tongue, Chaucer's English shows the way to more flexible, inchoate, and spontaneous forms of expression where rules of genre have yet to harden.

Drama, *Stress*, and Adaptation

Exception must be made for Shakespeare as a brilliant early reader of Chaucer. Such is the intensity of his engagement that familiarity with Shakespeare makes us better readers of Chaucer. This holds true for Shakespeare's large-scale reworkings in *A Midsommer Nights Dreame* (*c.*1594–5), *Troylus and Cressida* (*c.*1602), and *Two Noble Kinsmen* (with John Fletcher, based on *The Knight's Tale*, *c.*1613). But it is more locally true, since many 'reaction shots' on the Shakespearean stage find counterparts in Chaucer. Consider this line from the first scene of *A Midsommer Nights Dream*:

THESEUS Come, my Hyppolyta: what cheare my love?   *cheer*
(1.1.122)

Theseus has here been deliberating (absent-mindedly, he says) on love suits, and has just threatened Hermia with a death sentence, or life in a nunnery, for disobeying her father. Hippolyta, sometime Queen of the Amazons, conquered by Theseus and brought forcibly to Athens, gets no line in this scene. The actress playing her thus has only that small gap between sentences to work with; the Theseus-actor then reacts to whatever facial and bodily expression ('What cheer, my love? *What's up with you*?') she chooses to muster. Many equivalent moments, when off-script reaction is inferable from what is on the page, can be found in Chaucer. Here in the *Wife of Bath's Tale*, for example, Queen Guenevere extends *provisional* hope of pardon to the knight-rapist:

I grante thee lyf, *if* thou kanst tellen me	*you can tell me*
What thyng it is that wommen moost desiren.	*want most*
BE WAR, and keep thy nekke-bone from iren!	*careful from the axe*

(3.904–6; emphases added)

Again, we can infer off-script reaction between sentences: Guenevere sees that the young man is about to answer her life-or-death question ('what do women most desire?') *right away*, without consultation, so she drops down on him quickly, just ahead of the axe. The Wife of Bath herself, in the course of her unstoppable prologue, builds in her own reaction shots: to those outraged by discussion of genital functions she asks, expecting no answer, 'sey ye no?' The Host, seeing that his banter has upset the Physician, says 'Seyde I nat wel?' (6.311). Dramatic effect in Chaucer demands choice of *stress*, landing heavily (as in Shakespeare) on words most crucial for intelligibility:

On *every* wrong a man may nat be wreken.   *may not be revenged*
Lerneth to suffre, or elles, so moot I goon,   *or else, I tell you*
Ye *shul* it lerne, wher so ye wol or noon.   *whether you like it or not*

(*CT* 5.776–8)

Sometimes this can be a single word, as with the Pardoner:

For though *myself* be a ful vicious man,   *am full of vices*
A moral tale yet I yow telle kan
Which I am wont to preche for to wynne.   *preach profit*

(6.459–61)

Sometimes, as with the *Merchant's Tale*, stresses downshift from very strong ('Strugle!') to less certain ('thoughte') as emotions modulate. May explains that she has stage-managed struggling up a pear tree with young Damian to help heal old January's eyesight:

'*Strugle?*' quod he, 'Ye, algate in it wente!   *anyways*
God yeve yow bothe on shames deth to dyen!   *give shameful death*
He *swyved* thee; I *saugh* it with myn yen'.   *fucked saw my eyes*

(4.2376–8)

But later:

   ...me *thoughte* he dide thee so.

   (4.2386)

'Strugle' at 4.2376 is followed by a question mark in the *Riverside Chaucer* and by an exclamation in Penguin: another reminder that interpretation begins with choices made in editing from the manuscript. In texts conceived for reading aloud, such as this one, choices of *stress* must be

125

strongly made, and in advance. The better these choices, the more audiences will understand. Teachers of Chaucer must thus mark up their texts in their closets before advancing to the classroom or stage.

Many Chaucerian tales possess qualities of dramatic structure that adapt readily to the stage. The *Miller's Tale* excels here, since a cry from one site of action ('Help! Water! Water!') spurs misinterpretation, and then drastic action ('Allas, now comth Nowelis flood!') at another (1.3815–18). The best adaptation of this Oxford scene was made by an Oxford don and dramaturg, Nevill Coghill, whose closing couplet is especially good:

> And Nicholas is scalded in the towte.
> This tale is doon, and God save al the rowte!
>
> (1.3853–4)
>
> And Nicholas is branded on the bum
> And God bring all of us to Kingdom Come.

Coghill capped a long career in college drama in 1968 with a musical stage version of *CT* that played for five years in London before touring to Broadway, Europe, and Australia. Focus on Chaucerian bawdy in 1968 established the production as *risqué* but essentially safe for public performance. Judgements of ethical and moral safety, however, continue to evolve. Rapid sexual 'seduction' in the *Reeve's Tale* raises issues of sexual consent that cannot now be satisfied, for students, by referring to conventions of low-life comic drama, or *fabliau*: the student John leaps on the sleeping Malyne 'er [before] she myghte espie', when it was 'to[o] late for to crie' (1.4195–6). Intelligent dramatic productions test such shifting limits. Mike Poulton's 2006 two-part *CT*, which opened at the Swan Theatre, Stratford-upon-Avon, before transferring to London and the wider world, featured a *Prioress's Tale* in which the actors playing Jews wore caricature masks with long noses. The actors playing Christians, wearing no masks, spent much time chanting by torchlight, evoking the Prioress's liturgically enveloped convent world. Darkness and the centralization of space intensified these effects. The audience was thus caught between identification (with the beauties of Anglican choral tradition) and denial (of Christian anti-Semitism). Such paralysis was solved *theatrically* by moving on to the *Nun's Priest's Tale*: bring on the dancing chickens, curtain, end of Part I, ice creams. This is a Chaucerian strategy. The Ellesmere order of *CT* sees the goofy *Tale of Sir Thopas*, rather than the *Nun's Priest's Tale*, follow the Prioress, but the *effect* is the same: comic performing releases the audience from reflective sobriety (7.692); ethical misgivings drift away, but never quite disperse.

Changes of performing space continually test text, players, audiences, and social *mores*. Mike Poulton's *Prioress's Tale* took on quite different resonances when transferred from Stratford-upon-Avon and London to the Eisenhower Theatre, Kennedy Center, Washington, DC. In Almagro, Spain, the bare bums of his *Miller's Tale* ran into trouble in a Dominican cloister, forcing a change of venue.

Internationalizing Chaucer: Scotland, Kynaston

Crucial first steps in internationalizing Chaucer were taken by James I of Scotland (1394–1437) as he returned to his homeland in 1424 carrying *The Kingis Quair*. This dream poem 'King's Book' in rhyme royal, inspired by reading Chaucer and Boethius during long years of English captivity, sparked greater diversity in Scottish poetics, especially in a group formerly known as 'Scottish Chaucerians': Robert Henryson (d. *c*.1490), whose *Testament of Cresseid* helped colour the disease-ridden world of Shakespeare's *Troylus and Cressida*; William Dunbar (*c*.1460–*c*.1513–30), anti-marriage polemicist; Gavin Douglas (*c*.1474–1522), whose *Aeneid* translation achieved what Chaucer could only dream of in his *House of Fame*; and Sir David Lyndsay (*c*.1486–1555), herald and social satirist. In 1633, Sir Francis Kynaston, esquire of the body to Charles I of England, published a parallel text of Latin and English poems celebrating the king's journey to Scotland for his coronation. Two years later, he published a parallel text of *Troilus and Criseyde*, Books I–II, with three stanzas of Chaucer's Middle English set out in black Gothic type on the right side of each page, and Kynaston's own Latin translation in italic script on the left—also, amazingly, in rhyme royal (Figure 15).

The suggestion of this layout—that the contemporary, italic qualities of Kynaston's Latin newly illuminate archaic, Gothic Chaucer—is taken up by many of the commendatory verses, written by Kynaston's friends, that preface his volume. 'Homebred *Chaucer*', says William Barker, 'unto us was such / As if he had bin written in High Dutch'. Chaucer's critics, before Kynaston, never made the effort to appreciate him: 'because they are lazie', says Barker, '*Chaucer's* Rude'. But Chaucer's 'seeming rudenesse', says Thomas Reade, was merely a matter of 'outward hew': which is to say the

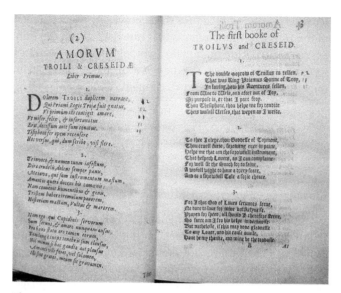

Figure 15 Francis Kynaston, *Amorum Troili et Creseidæ*. An early reader of this copy (BL 81.a.27) has experimented briefly with counting syllables.

outlandish, rustic-medieval garb in which his verse (as represented by the Gothic type) comes dressed. Kynaston's Latin across the page here *licenses* the Middle English, like a courtly figure leading an outlandish, half-forgotten relative back into polite society.

Samuel Evans, eager to hear '*Chaunticleare/*Crowe latin', urges Kynaston on to yet more translating; the Pope and his cardinals would then surely make Chaucer 'Canonicall'. It is thanks to Kynaston, William Cartwright argues, 'that wee / Read *Chaucer* now without a Dictionary'. Which is ridiculous:

Chaucer was not difficult for these university-educated men of the 1630s. But the *posture* is that true Englishness can only be recognized, internationally, through Latin. Chaucer's tongue, grown strange, can be restored, made 'ours' again, only by putting on Kynaston's garment:

> ... Hee, that hitherto
> Was dumbe to strangers, and's owne Country too,   *his own*
> Speakes plainely now to all; being more oure owne
> Ev'n hence, in that thus made to Aliens knowne.   *from now on*

Globalizing Chaucer: Argentina to Wales, London

Chaucer foresaw his own language, like all mother tongues, falling away from future generations (see p. 66), but its rate of fall has been especially dramatic: English has changed with exceptional speed when compared, say, to Italian. Yet English has effectively replaced Latin as a world language; Kynaston and company backed the wrong horse. In recent decades, English's global reach has fuelled fascination across the globe with Chaucer as an originating poet. The online *Global Chaucers* project continues to log and link translations and adaptations across the world, from Argentina to Wales via Estonia and Serbia. Chaucer can now be read in Afrikaans and Esperanto, Frisian and Hebrew. There is now a Swedish *Canterburysägner* and an Icelandic *Kantaraborgarsögur*. In the mountains of Iranian Azerbaijan, a region with sedimented Armenian, Jewish, and Assyrian histories, Alireza Mahdipour has translated Chaucer into Farsi verse (published at Tehran in three volumes, 2009). Just the *Squire's Tale*, with its tale of Cambyuskan (most likely

Genghis Khan), has been published in Mongolian, and it is (I have found) possible to debate that tale's sources with an Uzbek barber on Mount Scopus, Jerusalem. Israelis and Palestinians soon become adept readers of Chaucer because his language is reliably phonetic: a *knight* in Middle English is a *knyght* and not, as in modern English, a *nite*. It is through *sound* that Chaucer's most exciting futures likely lie, with audio files complementing, if not edging out, the printed page.

Such globalizing makes us appreciate anew that Chaucer's poetic fictions really do cover a remarkable geographical range, 'from Denmark to India', as the Wife of Bath says (3.824), and way beyond (map). This also facilitates return to Chaucer as a London poet, with London freshly appreciated as a global city. Some of the most compelling pages of Paul Strohm's *Poet's Tale* detail Chaucer's years at the Customs House, money hub of the international economy, as formatively creative. Peter Ackroyd's Londons are darkly destructive, forever reinventing themselves; his claustrophobic *Clerkenwell Tales*, with each of its twenty-two chapters named after a Chaucerian pilgrim, is a pilgrimage text that never leaves the city. David Dabydeen, who moved from Guyana to London aged thirteen, tells in his novel *The Intended* of attempts to master *Troilus and Criseyde* by way of impressing nice, white, A-level student Janet. But it is his later engagement with percussive and unsmoothed alliterative metre, as in *Sir Gawain*, that leads him to the coruscating lyrics of *Slave Song* (1984); faraway Middle English resonates, to magical effect, with faraway (but close to home) Guyanese creole. Darcus Howe, on coming from Trinidad to

Map of Chaucer's Europe c.1400.

London at eighteen, found the canon of English poetry laid out on Brixton streets (as conceived by Victorian town planners): Chaucer, Spenser, Shakespeare, Milton. Later, in walking these streets (much troubled c.1970), Howe imagines

that 'Chaucer's ghost breaks silence as he recites the *Complaint of Troilus*:

> *From thennesforth he rideth up and doun,*
> *And everything come him to remembrance,*

> As he rode forby places of the town
> In which he whilllom had all his pleasiance.

(p. 170)

The odd orthographic presentation of *T&C* 5.561–4 here perhaps owes something to *Time Out* typesetting (corrected in later editions), or perhaps conveys Howe's quoting from memory. Consistency of spelling is, in any case, yet one more thing that modern editors, as late Victorians, impose upon medieval texts. Howe's evocation of Chaucer as part of dense London cultural texture carries forward in *The Wife of Bath Speaks in Brixton Market* by Jamaican dub poet Jean Binta Breeze (Figure 16).

This may be read in the collection *The Arrival of Brighteye* (2000), but there is an immensely rewarding video (2006), beautifully edited and produced, that sees the poet performing her couplets as she walks through the market, astonishing the locals. Patience Agbabi's 'Wife of Bafa' may also be viewed as performing video or read as part of a collection, in this case *Telling Tales* (2014). Agbabi's Wife, Mrs Alice Ebi Bafa from Nigeria, confounds her fifth husband:

> He wanted ten children to pass my hip
> But I learnt how to wield de whip.

(p. 33)

Also from Nigeria is Constance of the *Man of Law's Tale*, as adapted by Olivia Hetreed for the six-part BBC *CT* series. Constance, as played by Nikki Amuka-Bird, is first seen washed up as a traumatized refugee at Chatham docks—which, before closing in 1984, had supplied royal fleets

Figure 16 Jean Binta Breeze.

with warships for over 400 years. Constance is fervently Christian, and this soon sets her apart from post-religious, mainstream English society. No mother-in-law, we soon see, can be quite as wicked as a middle-class Englishwoman whose son seems bent on unsuitable marriage. Like all excellent adaptations, this beautifully filmed and acted *Man of Law's Tale* sees Chaucer 'coming home' to find a contemporary England both familiar and strange.

Poetry, Finally

Chaucer long worried about *poesye* in English but came to believe, by the end of *T&C*, that he had achieved it (5.1790; and p. 69 in this volume). In 2011, a memorial was laid at his corner of Westminster Abbey, Poets' Corner, for a fellow poet who found that only Chaucer, and specifically *T&C*, could frame his ill-starred love affair. Love of Chaucer as a common bond between Sylvia Plath and Ted Hughes, as recorded by his *Birthday Letters*, is attested by a poem called simply 'Chaucer'. This sees Plath mounting a stile during a walk across the fields to Grantchester: a key Chaucerian *limen* (p. 114 in this volume) en route to a literary place frequented by the Bloomsbury group. Plath's *sostenuto* declamation of Chaucer runs on and on, astonishing a herd of cows. Having begun with *GP*, she then modulates to the Wife of Bath—her favourite character, Hughes says, in all of literature. Hughes himself, much given to astrological calculation for serious life events, had reached for Chaucer when remembering his first sighting of Plath on 26 February 1956. The first half of 'St Botolph's' in *The Birthday Letters* details the alignment of planets at that fateful meeting, with 'our Chaucer' serving as commentator and guide (before curling up to stay home with Dante). The second half moves to *innamoramento*, the moment of falling in love. The title and hero of Chaucer's Italian source is *Filostrato*, 'love-struck', and his English counterpart is similarly smitten (or 'stiken') by 'fixe and depe impressioun' of a woman, at first sight (1.297–8). Hughes is similarly slain from the start, although able (like Chaucer) to register the very specific gestures, expressions, and hand movements that knocked him flat. His Criseyde is a little more designing than Chaucer's, since Plath (he says) contrived to be on that dance floor, and to be seen by him. Hughes and Plath were married on Bloomsday, less than four months later, and went on to live out the greatest poetic *tragedie* of the age.

Lavinia Greenlaw's *A Double Sorrow* (2014), a title taken from *T&C*'s opening line, is a sequence of just over 200 seven-line poems, lightly rhymed as a modern variant of *rhyme royal*. Each poem is free-standing and yet responds with great focus to a specific section of Chaucer's poem: line numbers to *T&C* are given, encouraging us to keep both poems in mind, on parallel tracks. *A Double Sorrow* does to *T&C* what Chaucer did to *Il Filostrato*, and Greenlaw clearly senses herself in a line of adaptation leading back through Benoît's *Roman de Troie* into classical antiquity. She is also Chaucerian in not fearing to foreground herself in the telling of her own poetry; Chaucerian narrators are partial, partisan, and never omniscient.

In *The Cachoeira Tales* (2005), poet Marilyn Nelson tells how she won a Fellowship enabling a group of fellow

'Americans of slave descent' to travel to 'some place sanctified by the Negro soul'. Nelson takes *CT* as her formal and metrical model, while questioning its structures: where, to begin with, is a fitting site for African-American pilgrimage? Zimbabwe, where Anglican Bernard Mizeki was martyred, proves too expensive. Senegal? Jamaica, or Trinidad? Finally, her *fellowship* settles on the church of Senhor do Bonfim, or Lord of the Good End, a site in the Bahia region of Brazil. This is a sacred site for Candomblé, a religion passed on by enslaved African priests between 1549 and 1850 and part-integrated with local Brazilian Catholicism. Issues of spiritual and cultural syncretism recur for Nelson and her band of African-American pilgrims. They do eventually make a time-compressed visit to their avowed destination, in the hurried manner of modern travellers. The most compelling site of contemplation, however, is the ocean itself, 'the blue Atlantic', which is, Nelson says, 'a bone highway' (p. 36). This vision of loss is balanced by the integration of her *fellowship* into the local Brazilian milieu, with a meal for thirty celebrated with music and dancing. This is the first version of a Chaucerian *compaignye*, to my knowledge, not punctiliously to separate itself from fellowship found on the road.

Caroline Bergvall, part-French and part-Norwegian, is a poet who writes and performs in English. Her artistic practice thus *embodies* Chaucer, since Chaucer, too, worked through an evolving amalgam of French and Germanic elements. As a non-native practitioner, Bergvall is especially attentive to ways in which every English sentence sees medieval elements bubbling to the surface and emerging from the mouth (as with *mouth*, from Old Saxon and cognate with Old Frisian *mūth*). She thus speaks of a *midden* (a term deriving from Old Norse) of language, a sedimented refuse heap, where arcane and archaic forms rise continuously to the surface. The strangeness of modern English spelling (*the*: a word written with a thorn or þ for *th* until the fourteenth century) and pronunciation (*the*: voiced as the tongue moves back *into* the throat, difficult for non-natives) often passes unnoticed. Such variety of linguistic form, attesting to great cultural depth and geographical breadth, is smoothed away, Bergvall proposes, by corporate-speak, the deadening language of in-flight magazines. In a series of experimental poems, Bergvall allows medieval forms and spellings to rise from the deep, co-existing with modern usage. The first of the five 'Shorter Chaucer Tales' in her collection *Meddle English*, called 'The Host Tale', hoovers up lines and phrases from throughout Chaucer that concern eating and drinking. This initial, framing act of *assembly* epitomizes what Chaucer's pilgrims assemble for at the Tabard in *CT*: eating and drinking. Next comes 'The Summer Tale', which tells of a papal fondness for ice cream:

> The last Papa Pope Johannes Paulus Tweye,
> a preest holy and gay,
> used to have tubs of his favourite flavour, marron glacé,
> delivered to his summer residence.
> Thanked be God, in wele and habundaunce!
>
> (p. 28, ll. 7–11)

Bergvall here celebrates the plasticity of medieval rhyming, plus verbal shifts in meaning over time ('holy and gay').

Pressure of metre and rhyme force a nasal, French-style pronunciation of 'residence'; the final line is a straight lift from *The Summoner's Tale* (3. 1723). The poem persists with the ice cream theme humorously to evoke Benedict XVI's visit to Poland. The poem following, 'The Franker Tale', takes a darker turn in considering a papal Letter to Women. 'The Not Tale' lays bare *CT*'s mightiest example of a single trope, *occultatio*, talking about something while insisting that you will *not* talk about it (as Chaucer's Knight will *not* talk about Arcite's funeral, 1.2919–66; and see p. 75 in this volume). Finally, 'The Fried Tale (London Zoo)' gives us London of the financial markets, where the texting-talk of two ill-educated young traders repeats the vagaries of medieval spelling, but not in a good way. Bergvall acknowledges, in her epigraph, a debt to Russell Hoban's *Riddley Walker* (1980), a novel inspired by a medieval wall painting in Canterbury Cathedral. Set some two millennia into the future, *Riddley Walker* evokes a world after nuclear war where word meanings have shifted and transcriptions are imperfect.

Print serves Bergvall well, given her use of medieval spellings, but her work must also be heard—and, if possible, seen. As a Franco-Norwegian performer of English, I have suggested, Bergvall *bodies forth* Chaucer with peculiar authenticity. As her two 'pope' tales make plain, however, such 'embodiment' is rebellious and difference-making, a development carried further in her 2008 chapbook *Alyson Singes* (her 'Wife of Bath'). Bergvall's work is perhaps best first approached, and most easily accessed, via audio files, if not through live performance. Her voicing of poetry, fed by Scandinavian and French intonations and augmented by some study of Middle English phonetics, gives us a strange new Chaucer of retro-futurity. Her more recent work in *Drift* (2014) voyages yet further afield in English, afloat on a language mass associated with Anglo-Saxon and Nordic sea-faring literatures. Here changes in meaning through time are visually represented, through video, by the drift of words across a screen.

Bergvall recognizes that *drift* is currently a matter of life or death for desperate people heading into the Mediterranean. In July 2016, she took part in *Refugee Tales*, a collaborative project involving new forms of Chaucerian tale-telling and a walk from Canterbury to London. Fourteen authors, including Patience Agbabi and Ali Smith, have also combined to produce a book called *Refugee Tales*, reworkings of pilgrim narrative featuring immigrants subject to indefinite detention. The march from Canterbury to London, which may become an annual event, reverses *CT* in moving from a time-honoured religious centre to the heart of English political power (although it was the Crown that reached out from Westminster to destroy Becket's shrine at Canterbury in 1538). As a poet struggling to achieve *poetrie* in English before English and its literary genres have stabilized, Chaucer appears antithetical to the kind of poet of robust virtues celebrated in 1850, or 1900 (500 years *post mortem*). But now his time has come. *The Tale of Januarie*, a fully staged opera performed at the Guildhall School, London, in 2017 and funded by a 'Cross-Language Dynamics' grant, proves protean Chaucerian *patois* to be more singable, librettist Stephen Plaice says, than modern English. The extraordinary growth of translations worldwide since 2000 suggests new esteem for Chaucer as the poet of an unfinished Englishness ripe for translation, adaptation, and local variation. His encyclopaedic interests recognize no barriers between arts and sciences. His dramatic qualities, appreciated by adaptors from Shakespeare to Pasolini, await new forms and theatres of performance. The wonderful *sound* and poetic power of his language, his Middle English, will continue to spread through audio and video technologies, inspiring new voices in new places.

TIMELINE: A WELL-DOCUMENTED LIFE

We know a great deal about Chaucer's life and movements because he was a royal or civil servant; there are currently 495 known life-records.

*c.*1340–3	Born on north bank of Thames, London, to John Chaucer and Agnes, *née* Copton.
1346–7	Siege of Calais by Edward III; Order of the Garter founded soon after.
1348	Bubonic plague reaches London; kills one in three across Europe.
1350	Christian (Catholic) Jubilee year; Boccaccio, completing his *Decameron*, first meets Petrarch.
1357	Gifted 2*s.* 6*d.* for 'necessaries at Christmas' in household of Elizabeth de Burgh, Countess of Ulster and wife of Lionel (son of Edward III).
1359–60	Serves with Prince Lionel in king's army. Captured near Reims (defended by poet Guillaume de Machaut) and then ransomed.
1360	Serves peace process in carrying letters between Calais and England. Treaty of Calais signed on 24 October, enabling nine-year truce.

1361–6	Prince Lionel, in Ireland, imposes *Statutes of Kilkenny* to counter Hibernization of English colonists; Chaucer's whereabouts unknown.
1365/6	Marries 'Philippa Pan', a knight's daughter from Hainault serving Philippa, queen to Edward III. Her sister Katherine Swynford will become mistress (*c.*1370) and third wife (1396) to John of Gaunt.
	Father dies, mother remarries; travels to Navarre on pilgrimage (Santiago de Compostella) and/or war-related business.
1367	Enters household of Edward III as *esquire*; son Thomas likely born this year.
1368–70	Travels and possibly fights in service of Edward III. Prince Lionel marries daughter of Bernabò Visconti, despot of Milan, in May 1368, with Petrarch present, and dies soon after.
1372–3	Travels to Genoa and then Florence on trade and military mission.
1373–80	Death of great authors in Italy: Bridget of Sweden (1373), Petrarch (1374), Boccaccio (1375), and Catherine of Siena (1380); Machaut, poet and composer, dies at Reims (1377).
1374–86	Controller of customs, port of London.
1377	Accession of Richard II; Chaucer is in France to help negotiate his marriage.
1378	Negotiates with Bernabò Visconti at Milan, and Sir John Hawkwood (English *condottiere*).
	Western schism sees England side with Roman pope, and Scotland with French rival.
1380	Released from *raptus* (rape or abduction) charges by Cecily Champain; son Lewis born.
1381	Anti-war, anti-taxation protesters occupy London for several weeks in June; vicious reprisals. Chaucer's

	mother dies; Anne of Bohemia, daughter of Holy Roman Emperor Charles IV, travels to England and marries Richard II in January 1382.
1384	Death of theologian, social theorist, and translator John Wycliffe.
1386	MP for Kent. Falls from grace, losing Aldgate dwelling and customs-house position.
1387	Philippa Chaucer, latterly spending little time with her spouse, dies.
1388	Nicholas Brembre, sometime mayor of London, and Thomas Usk, scrivener and author of *The Testament of Love*, executed.
1389–91	Clerk of King's Works, responsible for upkeep of royal properties.
1389	Ottomans defeat Serbs at Kosovo.
1391	Pogroms and forced conversions of Jews in Spain.
1394	Granted royal annuity of £20 for life; Anne of Bohemia dies.
1395	Chronicler and poet Jean Froissart returns to London for first time since death of Queen Philippa in 1369.
1396	Combined Christian armies routed by Ottomans at Nicopolis on lower Danube.
1397	Oton de Granson, admired knight-poet, dies duelling in Savoy.
1399	Deposition and then murder of Richard II; Chaucer leases a house at Westminster Abbey.
1400	Annuities renewed by Henry IV; he dies in October, buried at Westminster Abbey.

FURTHER READING

Listed here are some resources for the further study of Chaucer, along with works referenced in this book, or especially influential to it. The edition followed in this book is: Geoffrey Chaucer, *The Riverside Chaucer*, ed. Larry Benson, new Foreword by Christopher Cannon (Oxford: Oxford University Press, 2008).

Ackroyd, Peter, *The Clerkenwell Tales* (London: Chatto and Windus, 2003).

Aesop's Fables, tr. Laura Gibbs (Oxford: Oxford University Press, 2008).

Agbabi, Patience, *Telling Tales* (Edinburgh: Canongate, 2014).

Akbari, Suzanne Conklin, *Idols in the East: European Representations of Islam and the Orient* (Ithaca, NY: Cornell University Press, 2009).

The Anglo-Saxon World: An Anthology, tr. Kevin Crossley-Holland (Oxford: Oxford University Press, 2009).

Bal, Mieke (ed.), *The Artemisia Files: Artemisia Gentileschi for Feminists and Other Thinking People* (Chicago, IL: University of Chicago Press, 2005).

Barber, Richard W., *The Life and Campaigns of the Black Prince: From Contemporary Letters, Diaries, and Chronicles, including Chandos Herald's 'Life of the Black Prince'* (Woodbridge: Boydell, 1997).

Barr, Helen, *Transporting Chaucer* (Manchester: Manchester University Press, 2014).

Barrington, Candace, *American Chaucers* (New York: Palgrave Macmillan, 2007).

Barron, Caroline M., *London in the Later Middle Ages: Government and People 1200–1500* (Oxford: Oxford University Press, 2005).

Benoît de Sainte-Maure, *Roman de Troie*, in R. K. Gordon, tr. and intro., *The Story of Troilus: as told by Benoît de Sainte-Maure, Giovanni Boccaccio, Geoffrey Chaucer, and Robert Henryson*, Medieval Academy Reprints for Teaching (Toronto: University of Toronto Press, 1978).

Bergvall, Caroline, *Alyson Singes* (New York: Belladonna, 2008).

Bergvall, Caroline, *Drift* (New York: Nightboat Books, 2014).

Bergvall, Caroline, *Meddle English. New and Selected Texts* (New York: Nightboat Books, 2011).

Boccaccio, Giovanni, *Concerning Famous Women*, ed. and tr. Virginia Brown (Cambridge, MA: Harvard University Press, 2001). Translated from the Latin autograph manuscript of *De mulieribus claris*.

Boccaccio, Giovanni, *The Decameron*, rev. edn, tr. G.H. McWilliam (London: Penguin, 1995).

Boccaccio, Giovanni, *The Fates of Illustrious Men*, tr. and abridged by Louis Brewer Hall (New York: Ungar, 1965).

Boccaccio, Giovanni, *Tutte le opere*, ed. Vittore Branca, 10 vols in 11 (Milan: Mondadori, 1964–98).

Boethius, *The Consolation of Philosophy*, tr. Peter Walsh (Oxford: Oxford University Press, 2008).

Boitani, Piero and Jill Mann (eds), *The Cambridge Companion to Chaucer*, 2nd edn (Cambridge: Cambridge University Press, 2003).

Bowers, John M. (ed.), *The Canterbury Tales: Fifteenth-Century Additions and Continuations* (Kalamazoo, MI: Medieval Institute Publications, 1992). http://d.lib.rochester.edu/teams/publication/bowers-canturbury-tales-fifteenth-century-continuations-and-additions.

Breeze, Jean 'Binta', 'The Wife of Bath in Brixton Market', in *The Arrival of Brighteye and Other Poems* (Bloodaxe Books: Newcastle-upon-Tyne, 2000), 62–4.

Butler, Judith, *Gender Trouble: Feminism and the Subversion of Identity* (London: Routledge, 1990).

Butterfield, Ardis (ed.), *Chaucer and the City* (Woodbridge: Boydell and Brewer, 2006).

Butterfield, Ardis, *The Familiar Enemy: Chaucer, Language, and Nation in the Hundred Years War* (Oxford: Oxford University Press, 2009).

Cannon, Christopher, *From Literacy to Literature: England, 1300–1400* (Oxford: Oxford University Press, 2016).

Cannon, Christopher, *The Making of Chaucer's English: A Study of Words* (Cambridge: Cambridge University Press, 1998).

Chaucer, Geoffrey, *The Canterbury Tales*, ed. Jill Mann (London: Penguin, 2005).

Chaucer, Geoffrey, *The Canterbury Tales*, an adaptation in two parts by Mike Poulton (London: Nick Herne Books, 2005).

Chaucer, Geoffrey, *The Canterbury Tales*, translated into modern English by Nevill Coghill [1951] (London: Penguin, 2003).

Chaucer, Geoffrey, *Complete Works*, ed. Rev. Walter W. Skeat, 7 vols (Oxford: Clarendon Press, 1894–7).

Chaucer, Geoffrey, *Selected Canterbury Tales*, tr. Alireza Mahdipour, 3 vols (Tehran: Cheshmeh Publishers, 2009).

Chaucer, Geoffrey, *Works: A Facsimile of the William Morris Kelmscott Chaucer, with the Original 87 Illustrations by Edward Burne-Jones* (London: CRW, 2007).

Chaucer Life-Records, ed. Martin M. Crowe and Clair C. Olson (Oxford: Clarendon Press, 1966).

Christine de Pisan, *Selected Writings*, ed. and tr. Renate Blumenfeld-Kosinski and Kevin Brownlee (New York: Norton, 1997).

Chute, Marchette, *Geoffrey Chaucer of England* (New York: E.P. Dutton, 1946).

Cohen, Jeffrey Jerome, *Stone: An Ecology of the Inhuman* (Minneapolis: University of Minnesota Press, 2015).

Cohen, Jeremy, *The Friars and the Jews: The Evolution of Medieval Anti-Judaism* (Ithaca: Cornell University Press, 1982).

Cooper, Helen, *The English Romance in Time: Transforming Motifs from Geoffrey of Monmouth to the Death of Shakespeare* (Oxford: Oxford University Press, 2004).

Cooper, Helen, *Oxford Guides to Chaucer: The Canterbury Tales*, 2nd edn (Oxford: Oxford University Press, 1996).

Copeland, Rita and Ineke Sluiter (eds), *Medieval Grammar and Rhetoric: Language Arts and Literary Theory, AD 300–1475* (Oxford: Oxford University Press, 2009).

Crane, Susan, *Animal Encounters: Contacts and Concepts in Medieval Britain* (Philadelphia: University of Pennsylvania Press, 2012).

Dabydeen, David, *The Intended* (London: Secker & Warburg, 1991).

Dabydeen, David, *Slave Song* (Mundelstrup: Dangaroo, 1984).

Dante Alighieri, *Il Convivio*, tr. Richard Lansing, parallel text (New York: Garland, 1990).

Dante Alighieri, *The Divine Comedy*, tr. Robin Kirkpatrick, parallel text, 3 vols (London: Penguin, 2006–7).

Dante Alighieri, *De Vulgari Eloquentia*, tr. Steven Botterill, parallel text (Cambridge: Cambridge University Press, 1996).

Davis, Isabel and Catherine Nall, *Chaucer and Fame: Reputation and Reception* (Cambridge: D.S. Brewer, 2015).

Davis, Kathleen and Nadia Altschul (eds), *Medievalisms in the Postcolonial World: The Idea of 'the Middle Ages' Outside Europe* (Baltimore, MD: Johns Hopkins University Press, 2009).

Davis, Norman, Douglas Gray, Patricia Ingham, and Anne Wallace-Hadrill (eds), *A Chaucer Glossary* (Oxford: Clarendon Press, 1979).

Deschamps, Eustache, *Selected Poems*, ed. Ian S. Laurie and Deborah M. Sinnreich-Levy, tr. David Curzon and Jeffrey Fiskin (London: Routledge, 2003).

Dinshaw, Carolyn, *Chaucer's Sexual Poetics* (Madison: University of Wisconsin Press, 1989).

Dinshaw, Carolyn, *How Soon Is Now? Medieval Texts, Amateur Readers, and the Queerness of Time* (Durham, NC: Duke University Press, 2012).

Douglas, Gavin, *Selections from Gavin Douglas*, ed. David F.C. Coldwell (Oxford: Clarendon Press, 1964).

Dunbar, William, *The Complete Works*, ed. John Conlee (Kalamazoo, MI: Medieval Institute Publications, 2004). http://d.lib.rochester.edu/teams/publication/conlee-dunbar-complete-works.

Eagleton, Terry, *Against the Grain: Essays 1975–1985* (London: Verso, 1986).

Ellis, Steve, *Chaucer at Large: The Poet in the Modern Imagination* (Minneapolis: University of Minnesota Press, 2000).

Fein, Susanna and David Raybin (eds), *Chaucer: Contemporary Approaches* (University Park, PA: Penn State University Press, 2009).

Froissart, Jean, *Chronicles*, tr. Geoffrey Brereton (London: Penguin, 1978).

Fumo, Jamie C., *The Legacy of Apollo: Antiquity, Authority, and Chaucerian Poetics* (Toronto: University of Toronto Press, 2010).

Gawain-Poet, *The Works of the Gawain Poet: Sir Gawain and the Green Knight, Pearl, Patience, Cleanness*, ed. Ad Putter and Myra Stokes (London: Penguin, 2014).

Geoffrey of Monmouth, *The History of the Kings of Britain*, tr. Michael A. Faletra (Peterborough, ON: Broadview, 2008).

Glassner, Ruth, *Averroes' Physics: A Turning Point in Medieval Natural Philosophy* (Oxford: Oxford University Press, 2009).

Gordon, R.K., tr. and intro., *The Story of Troilus: as told by Benoît de Sainte-Maure, Giovanni Boccaccio, Geoffrey Chaucer, and Robert Henryson*, Medieval Academy Reprints for Teaching (Toronto: University of Toronto Press, 1978).

Granson, Oton de, *Poésies*, ed. Joan Grenier-Winther (Paris: Champion, 2016).

Green, Richard Firth, *A Crisis of Truth: Literature and Law in Medieval England* (Philadelphia: University of Pennsylvania Press, 1998).

Green, Richard Firth, *Elf Queens and Holy Friars: Fairy Beliefs and the Medieval Church* (Philadelphia: University of Pennsylvania Press, 2016).

Greenlaw, Lavinia, *A Double Sorrow: Troilus and Criseyde* (London: Faber & Faber, 2015).

Gregorian chant, *Benedicta: Marian Chant from Norcia*, CD and MP3 download (De Montfort Music, 2015).

Guido delle Colonne, *Historia destructionis Troiae*, tr. M.E. Meek (Bloomington: Indiana University Press, 1974); see also Havely, *Chaucer's Boccaccio*, pp. 184–6.

Havely, N.R. (tr.), *Chaucer's Boccaccio: Sources of Troilus and the Knight's and Franklin's Tales* (Woodbridge: D.S. Brewer, 1980).

Heng, Geraldine, *Empire of Magic: Medieval Romance and the Politics of Cultural Fantasy* (New York: Columbia University Press, 2003).

Henry of Grosmont, Duke of Lancaster, *The Book of Holy Medicines*, tr. Catherine Batt (Tempe, AZ: ACMRS, 2014).

Henryson, Robert, *The Complete Works*, ed. David J. Parkinson (Kalamazoo, MI: Medieval Institute Publications, 2010).

http://d.lib.rochester.edu/teams/publication/parkinson-henryson-the-complete-works.

Heywood, Thomas, *Troia Britanica, or, Great Britaines Troy* [1609], facsimile (Hildesheim: Georg Olms Verlag, 1972).

Hoban, Russell, *Riddley Walker* (London: Bloomsbury, 2012).

Holsinger, Bruce, *A Burnable Book: A Novel* (New York: HarperCollins, 2014).

Horobin, Simon, *Chaucer's Language*, 2nd edn (Basingstoke: Palgrave Macmillan, 2013).

Howe, Darcus, 'Black Sabbath', in *Time Out London Walks*, vol. 1, 2nd edn (London: Penguin, 2002), 166–73.

Hsy, Jon, *Trading Tongues: Merchants, Multilingualism, and Medieval Literature* (Columbus: Ohio State University Press, 2013).

Hudson, Anne, *The Premature Reformation: Wycliffite Texts and Lollard History* (Oxford: Clarendon Press, 1998).

Hughes, Ted, *Birthday Letters* (London: Faber, 1998).

Ibn Battuta, *The Travels of Ibn Battutah*, tr. and abridged by Tim Mackintosh-Smith (London: Picador, 2003).

Ibn Khaldun, *The Muqaddimah: An Introduction to History*, ed. and abridged by N.J. Dawood, tr. F. Rosenthal (Princeton, NJ: Princeton University Press, 2015).

Jacobus de Voragine, *The Golden Legend*, tr. W.G. Ryan, intro. Eamon Duffy (Princeton, NJ: Princeton University Press, 2012).

King James I of Scotland, *The Kingis Quair*, in *The Kingis Quair and Other Prison Poems*, ed. Linne R. Mooney and Mary-Jo Arne (Kalamazoo, MI: Medieval Institute Publications, 2005).

http://d.lib.rochester.edu/teams/publication/mooney-and-arn-kingis-quair-and-other-prison-poems.

Jauss, H.R., *Toward an Aesthetic of Reception*, tr. Timothy Bahti (Minneapolis: University of Minnesota Press, 1982).

Joceline, Elizabeth, *The Mother's Legacy to her Unborn Child*, ed. Jean Le Drew Metcalfe (Toronto: University of Toronto Press, 2000).

Julian of Norwich, *Revelations of Divine Love*, tr. Barry Windeatt (Oxford: Oxford University Press, 2015).

Justice, Steven, 'Literary History', in *Chaucer: Contemporary Approaches*, ed. Susanna Fein and David Raybin (University Park, PA: Penn State University Press, 2009), 195–210.

Karnes, Michelle, *Imagination, Meditation, and Cognition in the Middle Ages* (Chicago, IL: University of Chicago Press, 2011).

Kempe, Margery, *The Book of Margery Kempe*, tr. Anthony Bale (Oxford: Oxford University Press, 2015).

Kruger, Stephen F., *Dreaming in the Middle Ages* (Cambridge: Cambridge University Press, 1992).

Kynaston, Francis, *Amorum Troili et Creseidæ libri duo priores anglico-latini* (Oxford: John Lichfield, 1635).

Langland, William, *The Vision of Piers Plowman*, B-Text, ed. A.V.C. Schmidt, 2nd edn (London: Dent, 1995).

Lanyer, Aemilia, *The Poems of Aemilia Lanyer: Salve Deus Rex Judaeorum*, ed. Susanne Woods (Oxford: Oxford University Press, 1993).

Lawler, Traugott and Ralph Hanna (eds), *Jankyn's Book of Wicked Wives*, 2 vols (Athens: University of Georgia Press, 1997–2014).

Leach, Elizabeth Eva, *Guillaume de Machaut: Secretary, Poet, Musician* (Ithaca, NY: Cornell University Press, 2011).

Leech-Wilkinson, Daniel, *Machaut's Mass: An Introduction* (Oxford: Clarendon Press, 1990).

Lydgate, John, Prologue to *The Siege of Thebes*, in John M. Bowers (ed.), *The Canterbury Tales: Fifteenth-Century Additions and Continuations* (Kalamazoo, MI: Medieval Institute Publications, 1992). http://d.lib.rochester.edu/teams/publication/bowers-canturbury-tales-fifteenth-century-continuations-and-additions.

Lyndsay, David, *Sir David Lyndsay, Selected Poems*, ed. Janet Hadley-Williams (Glasgow: Association for Scottish Literary Studies, 2000).

McDonald, Nicola, *Pulp Fictions of Medieval England: Essays in Popular Romance* (Manchester: Manchester University Press, 2004).

McGinnis, Jon, *Avicenna* (New York and Oxford: Oxford University Press, 2010).

Machaut, Guillaume de, *The Judgement of the King of Bohemia*, tr. R. Barton Palmer, parallel text (New York: Garland, 1984).

Machaut, Guillaume de, *The Judgement of the King of Navarre*, tr. R. Barton Palmer, parallel text (New York: Garland, 1988).

Machaut, Guillaume de, *Le livre dou voir dit* [*The Book of the True Poem*], tr. R. Barton Palmer, parallel text (New York: Garland, 1998).

Machaut, Guillaume de, *Messe de Notre Dame,* Ensemble Organum, CD (Harmonia Mundi, 2008).

Machaut, Guillaume de, *La prise d'Alexandrie* [*The Taking of Alexandria*], ed. R. Barton Palmer, parallel text (New York: Garland, 2002).

Machaut, Guillaume de, *Songs from Le voir dit*, CD (Hyperion, 2013).

Magoun, Francis P., *A Chaucer Gazetteer* (Chicago, IL: University of Chicago Press, 1961).

Malory, Sir Thomas, *Complete Works*, ed. Eugene Vinaver, 2nd edn (Oxford: Oxford University Press, 1971).

Mandeville, John, *The Book of Marvels and Travels*, tr. Anthony Bale (Oxford: Oxford University Press, 2012).

Mann, Thomas, *Death in Venice and Other Stories*, tr. David Luke (London: Vintage, 2003).

Marvin, William Perry, *Hunting Law and Ritual in Medieval England* (Cambridge: D.S. Brewer, 2006).

Mechain, Gwerful, see *Medieval Welsh Erotic Poetry*, ed. Daffyd Johnston, parallel text (Bridgend: Seren, 1998).

Minnis, Alastair, *The Cambridge Introduction to Chaucer* (Cambridge: Cambridge University Press, 2014).

Nelson, Marilyn, *The Cachoeira Tales and Other Poems* (Baton Rouge: Louisiana State University Press, 2005).

Nievergelt, Marco and Stephanie A. Viereck Gibbs (eds), *The Pèlerinage Allegories of Guillaume de Deguileville: Tradition, Authority, and Influence* (Cambridge: D.S. Brewer, 2013).

Ovid, *Metamorphoses*, tr. Charles Martin (New York: Norton, 2010).

Patterson, Lee W., 'Chaucerian Confession: Penitential Literature and the Pardoner', *Medievalia et Humanistica*, 7 (1976), 153–74.

Patterson, Lee W., 'Perpetual Motion: Alchemy and the Technology of the Self', *Studies in the Age of Chaucer*, 15 (1993), 25–57.

Pearsall, Derek, *The Life of Geoffrey Chaucer: A Critical Biography* (Oxford: Blackwell, 1992).

Pound, Ezra, *Personae. Collected Shorter Poems* [1926] (London: Faber & Faber, 2001).

Rashed, Roshdi, *Encyclopedia of the History of Arabic Science*, 3 vols (London: Routledge, 1996).

Refugee Tales, ed. David Herd and Anna Pincus (Manchester: Comma Press, 2016).

Rigby, Stephen H (ed.), *Historians on Chaucer* (Oxford: Oxford University Press, 2014).

The Romance of the Rose (Guillaume de Lorris, Jean de Meun, *Le Roman de la Rose*), tr. Frances Horgan (Oxford: Oxford University Press, 2008).

Rosenfeld, Jessica, *Ethics and Enjoyment in Late Medieval Poetry: Love After Aristotle* (Cambridge: Cambridge University Press, 2010).

Rubin, Miri, *Gentile Tales: The Narrative Assault on Late Medieval Jews* (New Haven, CT: Yale University Press, 1999).

Rubin, Miri (ed. and tr.), *The Life and Passion of William of Norwich* by Thomas of Monmouth (London: Penguin, 2014).

Ruggiers, Paul G. (ed.), *Editing Chaucer: The Great Tradition* (Norman, OK: Pilgrim Books, 1984).

St Erkenwald, ed. Ruth Morse (Cambridge: D.S. Brewer, 1975).

Savage, Anne and Nicholas Watson (trs.), *Anchoritic Spirituality: 'Ancrene Wisse' and Associated Works* (Mahwah, NJ: Paulist Press, 1991).

Seaman, Myra, Eileen Joy, and Nicola Masciandro (eds), *Dark Chaucer: An Assortment* (Brooklyn, NY: punctum books, 2012); open access http://punctumbooks.com.

Shakespeare, William, *The Complete Works. Original-Spelling Edition*, ed. Stanley Wells and Gary Taylor (Oxford: Clarendon Press, 1986).

Siege of Jerusalem, ed. Michael Livingston (Kalamazoo, MI: Medieval Institute Publications, 2004). http://d.lib.rochester.edu/teams/publication/livingston-siege-of-jerusalem.

The Song of Roland and Other Poems of Charlemagne, ed. and tr. Simon Gaunt and Karen Pratt (Oxford: Oxford University Press, 2016).

Statius, *Thebaid*, tr. Jane Wilson Joyce (Ithaca, NY: Cornell University Press, 2008).

Steiner, Emily, *Reading Piers Plowman* (Cambridge: Cambridge University Press, 2013).

Strohm, Paul, *The Poet's Tale. Chaucer and the Year that made* The Canterbury Tales (London: Profile Books, 2014).

Strohm, Paul, *Social Chaucer*, new edn (Cambridge, MA: Harvard University Press, 1994).

The Tale of Gamelyn, in *Robin Hood and Other Outlaw Tales*, ed. Stephen Knight and Thomas H. Ohlgren (Kalamazoo, MI: Medieval Institute Publications, 1997). http://d.lib.rochester.edu/teams.

Trigg, Stephanie, *Shame and Honor: A Vulgar History of the Order of the Garter* (Philadelphia: University of Pennsylvania Press, 2012).

Turner, Marion, *Chaucerian Conflict: Languages of Antagonism in Late Fourteenth-Century London* (Oxford: Clarendon Press, 2007).

Usk, Thomas, *The Testament of Love*, ed. R. Allen Shoaf (Kalamazoo, MI: Medieval Institute Publications, 1998).

Vergil, *Aeneid*, tr. Frederick Ahl, intro. Elaine Fantham (Oxford: Oxford University Press, 2007).

Wallace, David, *Chaucerian Polity* (Stanford, CA: Stanford University Press, 1999).

Wallace, David (ed.), *Europe: A Literary History, 1348–1418*, 2 vols (Oxford: Oxford University Press, 2016).

William of Malmesbury, *Gesta Regum Anglorum*, ed. and tr. R.A.B. Mynors, completed by R.M. Thomson and M. Winterbottom, 2 vols (Oxford: Oxford University Press, 1998–9), Latin with facing translation.

Wogan-Browne, Jocelyn et al. (eds), *Language and Culture in Medieval Britain: The French of England, c.1100–c.1500* (York: York Medieval Press, 2009).

Wyatt, Sir Thomas, *The Complete Poems*, ed. R.A. Rebholz (London: Penguin, 1997).

Yeats, W.B., *The Poems*, ed. Daniel Albright (London: Everyman, 1992).

Zeeman, Nicolette, 'The Gender of Song in Chaucer', *Studies in the Age of Chaucer*, 29 (2007), 141–82.

Original Sources Cited

Aberystwyth, National Library of Wales, MS Peniarth 392D (Hengwrt Chaucer). https://www.llgc.org.uk/?id=257.

Cambridge, Corpus Christi College, MS 61 (*T&C*), https://parkerweb.stanford.edu/parker/actions/page_turner.do?ms_no=61.

London, British Library, MS Harley 3647 (astronomical texts). http://www.bl.uk/manuscripts/FullDisplay.aspx?ref=Harley_MS_3647.

Oxford, Merton College, MS 259 (astronomical, including Alphonsine tables). https://www.merton.ox.ac.uk/library-and-archives.

San Marino, CA, Huntington Library, MS EL 26 C 9 (Ellesmere Chaucer). http://bancroft.berkeley.edu/digitalscriptorium/huntington/EL26C9.html.

Film, Video, Audio, Opera

Bergvall, Caroline. http://www.carolinebergvall.com.

Bergvall, Caroline, *Drift*. http://www.carolinebergvall.com/drift-performance.php.

Bergvall, Caroline, readings on PennSound. http://writing.upenn.edu/pennsound/x/Bergvall.php.

The Canterbury Tales (I Racconti di Canterbury), directed by Pier Paolo Pasolini (United Artists, 1972).

The Canterbury Tales (Ziji Productions for BBC, 2003). In order of broadcast: *Miller's Tale*, dir. John McKay; *Wife of Bath's Tale*, dir. Andy de Emmony; *Knight's Tale*, dir. Marc Munden; *Sea Captain's Tale* [*Shipman's Tale*], dir. John McKay; *Pardoner's Tale*, dir. Andy de Emmony; *Man of Law's Tale*, dir. Julian Jarrold. IMC VISION DVD on 2 discs.

Chaucer readings and discussions on PennSound (David Wallace). http://writing.upenn.edu/pennsound/x/Wallace.php.

Global Chaucers. https://globalchaucers.wordpress.com.

Hamlet, dir. Lawrence Olivier (Rank, 1948).

Historyteachers, *The Canterbury Tales* (mashup video using Ellesmere manuscript, sung to The Mamas and The Papas' 'California Dreamin'', lines from *GP* in Middle English). https://www.youtube.com/watch?v=vBa5nN_JyPk.

Refugee Tales. http://refugeetales.org.

The Seventh Seal, dir. Ingmar Bergman (AB Svensk Filmindustri, 1957).

The Tale of Januarie, music by Julian Philips, libretto by Stephen Plaice, Guildhall School of Music & Drama, performed 27 February–6 March 2017.

'Vogue', single and video by Madonna (Sire, Warner Brothers, 1990).

Zoolander, dir. Ben Stiller (Paramount, 2001).

Useful Websites and Web-Based Resources

Chaucer MetaPage: promotes and centralizes web-based resources. http://www.unc.edu/depts/chaucer/.

Digital Scriptorium, a consortium of libraries providing free online access to medieval manuscripts. http://bancroft.berkeley.edu/digitalscriptorium/.

eChaucer: includes link to Concordance, invaluable for studying use and frequency of particular words. https://machias.edu/faculty/necastro/chaucer/index.html.

Harvard Chaucer website: editions, reading instructions, and bibliography. http://chaucer.fas.harvard.edu.

The Latin Library: for quick reference to dozens of texts, no translations. http://www.thelatinlibrary.com/about.html.

Medieval Academy of America: excellent web resources. http://www.medievalacademy.org.

Medieval Manuscripts Blog, images from the British Library. http://britishlibrary.typepad.co.uk/digitisedmanuscripts/.

New Chaucer Society: meets biennially and supports all aspects of scholarship, including outreach to teachers; excellent resource page. https://newchaucersociety.org/resources/.

Open Access Companion to *CT*: exploratory, interactive guide for readers. http://www.opencanterburytales.com.

Visualizing Chaucer: artists and images through time. http://d.lib.rochester.edu/chaucer.

PUBLISHER'S ACKNOWLEDGEMENTS

We are grateful for permission to include the following copyright material in this book:

Extract from Terry Eagleton, *Against the Grain, 1975–1985* (London: Verso, 1986). Used with permission.

Extract from 'The Miller's Tale' in Chaucer, Geoffrey, *The Canterbury Tales*, translated into modern English by Nevill Coghill (London: Penguin, 2003), first published 1951, p 106. Copyright 1951 by Nevill Coghill. Copyright © the Estate of Nevill Coghill, 1958, 1960, 1975, 1977. Reproduced by permission of Penguin Books Ltd.

Extract from Darcus Howe, 'Black Sabbath', in *Time Out London Walks*, vol. 1, 2nd edition (London: Penguin, 2002), 166–73.

Extract from Caroline Bergvall, *Meddle English. New and Selected Texts* (Nightboat Books, 2011). Reprinted with permission of the author and Nightboat Books

Extract from Patience Agbabi's 'Wife of Bafa' © Patience Agbabi, 2014. Published in the UK by Canongate Books Ltd.

Publisher's Acknowledgements

The publisher and author have made every effort to trace and contact all copyright holders before publication. If notified, the publisher will be pleased to rectify any errors or omissions at the earliest opportunity.

INDEX

Index